Henry Tuckley

Forward March: Through Battle to Victory

Talks to Young People on Life and Success

Henry Tuckley

Forward March: Through Battle to Victory
Talks to Young People on Life and Success

ISBN/EAN: 9783744756129

Printed in Europe, USA, Canada, Australia, Japan

Cover: Foto ©ninafisch / pixelio.de

More available books at **www.hansebooks.com**

Forward March:

Through Battle to Victory.

Talks to Young People
on
Life and Success.

BY

REV. HENRY TUCKLEY,
Author of "Life's Golden Morning."

Forty Illustrations.

CINCINNATI: CRANSTON & STOWE.
NEW YORK: HUNT & EATON.

DEDICATION.

As a small token of my personal regard for him, and in grateful appreciation of his kindness to ministers of the gospel, his generous benefactions to children, his labors in behalf of young people, and the devoted service he has given for many years to the cause of wholesome literature, I dedicate this book on

Life and Success

to my honored friend,

AMOS SHINKLE,

A Christian gentleman whose best title of nobility is in his own name and character, and who, at the same time that he has been solving the problem of success in a satisfactory manner in his own life, has also, in the various ways indicated, done what he could to make many other lives successful.

H. T.

INTRODUCTION.

TO make palpable to young people the important fact that life is a battle which can only be won by the brave and true; to show, in the most forcible manner, that to those who exhibit these qualities victory is a foregone conclusion, but that the wicked, the worldly, the cowardly, and the indifferent can expect nothing save defeat; and to demonstrate, at the same time, that this fact of life being a battle, is one which, far from arousing fear or causing discouragement, should inspire us with enthusiasm and incite to the noblest efforts,— such are the purposes of this book. It is intended, in a word, to link arms with the young people's societies of the day, and to help these in preparing the rising generation for valiant service in the grand army of the future.

The military idea has been adopted, not only

because it correctly expresses the facts in the case, but for the additional reason that, to young people, it is always pleasing, and is very likely to prove impressive and convincing. One feature, which is sure to be welcome, is quite unusual in books of this kind. We refer to the notes, which, on almost every page, indicate so plainly what topic is under treatment. Another interesting feature is the illustrations. These are sure to be enjoyed; and when it has been observed that the renowned men whose portraits are given are held up as models, not in any general sense, excepting in a few instances, but only in the particular things to which distinct reference is made, we can safely leave the pictorial parts of the book to tell their own story and to teach their own stimulating lessons.

"Forward March" is similar in both style and aim to our other work, "Life's Golden Morning." The latter, however, deals chiefly with manners and conduct; whereas this, though no less practical than that, treats more fully of character and destiny, and shows in clearer and stronger light what is necessary to success in the highest meaning of that term.

The author flatters himself that there is nothing in the book contrary to either divine truth or human reason. Yet it was not written for theologians nor for profound philosophers. It was written for young people, our aim having been to adapt it in all respects to the tastes and needs of that interesting class. If these shall be attracted to it, and if, in reading what has been written, they shall be led to better views of life and duty, we shall have gained our object, and shall be deeply thankful.

THE AUTHOR.

CONTENTS.

I.
CHOOSING SIDES.

INTERESTING Situation of an Ancient People—What it means to live—The Period of Moral Helplessness—Human Incapacity covered by Divine Mercy—Starting out for Ourselves—The Choosing and Formative Period—Self-made Men not Exceptional—Does Opportunity make the Man?—The Chisel of Destiny—The Greatest Thing on Earth—Why Life is a Battle—Moral Neutrality not Possible—Choice limited to Two Sides—How Two Great Armies are recruited—Life's Dangerous Undertow—Importance of turning the Switch—Drifting toward the Rapids—Necessity of a Fixed and Worthy Aim—The Proper Time to Enlist—Importance of Right Beginnings—Of Two Courses, Which?—God's Service a Reasonable One—Urgent Call to Decision—An Ultimatum from Head-quarters—True Motives of a Worthy Life, ... PAGES 17-38

II.
THE FLAG WE FOLLOW.

AN Ancient Battle-hymn—A Sweet Singer and his Chief Musician—How Battle-hymns stimulate to Valor—Times which try the Soul—Victory only by doing

Duty—Use of Flags at Sea—Some who carry Satan's Flag—Two Flags which never harmonize—The Eloquence of Flags—Principles represented by the Flag we follow—A Flag which stands for Honesty, Purity, and Benevolence—The Standard of Moral Progress—The American Flag in 1812—How the Flag we follow has extended its Conquests—A Flag with a Mighty Future—Destiny of the Dark Continent—The American Flag in Siberia—What it means to have Heaven's Flag Above us—His Satanic Majesty and the Czar of Russia—A Flag which symbolizes Hope and Help for All—What we owe to the Flag we follow—"Don't let that Flag go down"—One who died for the Flag—Advantages of keeping our Colors flying, ... PAGES 39–62

III.
THE FOES WE FIGHT.

THE Great Opportunity of a Great Man—How Opposition should incite to Heroism—The Circus Maximus and its Lessons—What it means to be at Life's Threshold—Prizes offered in the Arena of Existence—Reputation Determined by Character—How to win a Commanding Position—A Grand Prize which is Possible to All—The Great Prize at the End—Victory only through Battle—Our Mightiest Foe, and his Methods of Assault—Lesson from the Great Bonaparte—A Fighting Chance to win—Why General Lee failed—How Industry discounts Genius—The Most Common Vice, What is it?—That Insidious Foe, Dishonesty—The True Way to Get on in Life—Awful Consequences of Impurity—Tenacity of Youthful Habits—Appalling Effects of Intemperance—Pledging the Modern Hannibals—How to achieve the Most Brilliant Conquests—Bright Side of the Battle of Life, ... PAGES 63–87

IV.

THE ALLIES WHO HELP US.

AN Inspiring Panorama—Anxious Question of a Trembling Youth—Wise Words from the Lips of Experience—First View of Life, What it reveals—An Eye-opening Prayer—Allies in Life's Battle whom we can not see—Lesson from the Sad Fate of Maximilian—The Mighty Government that backs us—Help from Angels, May we expect this?—The Great Question, How?—Celestial Forces on Terrestrial Battle-fields—Angelic Help not Adequate to Human Need—Our Chief Reliance in Life's Battle—Advantages of having God with us—Comparative Estimate of those for and against us—A Winning Battle-cry—What is Necessary to put God on our Side—The Great Strategic Point in Life's Battle—A Memorable Campaign, What it teaches—After Conversion, What?—Earthly Alliances which offer Help—Why we need the Church—Sterling Advice of an Old Sea-captain—Lesson from the Johnstown Flood—Another View of Life's Golden Morning—Helps to Success in Life, ... PAGES 89–112

V.

THE CAPTAIN WHO LEADS US.

THE Divine Purpose in Human Life—Earthly Honors in Contrast with Heavenly—The Chief End of Existence—Our Imperative Need of Jesus Christ—Prizes we may win by our Own Unaided Efforts—Success which means only Failure—Two Notable Lives, and what they teach—True Success only by Self-denial—What it means to enter the Army—Shouldering the Musket from Principle—First Requirement of the Captain who leads us—

Three Inspiring Examples—Noble Resolve of a Burmese Boatman—What our Captain has done for us—The Great Blot on Bonaparte's Escutcheon—How Battles were directed in the Late War—Peter the Great and Christ the Greatest—Advantage of Rising from the Ranks—Qualities of a Perfect Commander—Alexander and Hannibal—A Leader who is always in Front—"There's the Duke, God bless him"—Of Two Commanders, which shall have us?—How an Ancient City was saved—Contingency in which Life must be a Failure, ... PAGES 113-138

VI.

THE WEAPONS OF OUR WARFARE.

NECESSITY of a Good Equipment—Dreadful Foes whom we can not see—A call to Manfulness—That Noble Drummer-boy—Life's Emergencies, How to meet them—Decisive Moments in Great Battles—Why Some Days are Evil Days—How Evil Days may be made Good—Snatching Honor from the Jaws of Danger—Putting on the Armor—What our Helmet signifies—Valor in Battle, How to secure it—Stirring Address of a Wise General to his Troops—A Sure Antidote to Discouragement—Evil Thoughts, Two Methods of treating them—The Breastplate of Righteousness — Guarding the Steps, Why and How?—The Uses of Gospel Foot-gear—An Interesting Paradox—Moral Security, How obtained—The Shield we are to carry—How to resist Temptation—The Best Weapon in the Universe—Significant Conduct of Two English Rulers—Necessity of Watchfulness and Prayer—How a Memorable Battle was won—What it means to be fully equipped for Life's Warfare, ... PAGES 139-170

VII.

QUALITIES OF A GOOD SOLDIER.

ADVICE of a Veteran to Young Recruits—The Universal Desire of Young People -" Plenty of Room at the Top"—The Highest Form of Excellence—Striking Contrast between Two Kinds of Fame—Paramount Requirement of the Good Soldier—The Divine Methods of Recruiting—Hardships and Sacrifices of Army Life—Sublime Instances of Youthful Heroism—Life's Greatest Battlefield, Where is it?—Appeal of Pizarro to the Castilians—Facts to be remembered when Choice is exercised—The Soldier's First Lesson—Consequences of Failure in Life's Battle—The Only Path leading to Happiness—Nature and Effects of True Courage—The Quality we most need—Analysis of the Courage of Luther—The Martyrs and the Great Martyr—How to fit Ourselves for Hazardous Duties—Heroism on the Field of Battle—An Old Adage improved upon—Why Some People get on in the World—The Sad Consequences of not having Grit and Grip—The Strong Pull not Enough—Characteristic Remark of Abraham Lincoln—Great Lesson taught by a Great General, . PAGES 171–203

VIII.

THE VICTORY.

AFTER-THOUGHTS of the Glorified Christ—Small Things compared to Greater—Looking Backward—A Golden Thread of Encouragement—Duty and Destiny Linking Hands—A Mechanical Certainty, and what it suggests—The Trick of an Ancient General—An Augur we can trust—Battle-fields that are Sacred—The Greatest Conflicts of History—Christ's Triumph the Pledge and

Model of Ours—The "Big I" and "Little You" People—When the "Big I" is Proper—Discriminating Testimony of a Dying Minister—The Scene when the King comes in—Looking Forward—Pictures of Heaven by an Eye-witness—Significance of Some Striking Metaphors—The Glory which excelleth—Thoughts which should thrill us—After Crosses, the Crown—Things worth Remembering — At Life's Threshold again—The Divine Visitor—How to treat Him—Last Words.
PAGES, ... 205-239

ILLUSTRATIONS.

	PAGE.
STARTING OUT,	*Frontispiece.*
THE TWO WAYS,	Facing page 16
JOSHUA,	21
TAKING GOOD AIM,	26
STEERING BY THE CHART,	Facing page 32
THE FLAG WE FOLLOW,	Facing page 38
THE SIGN OF TRIUMPH,	49
A BRAVE STANDARD-BEARER,	55
JULIUS CÆSAR,	58
IN THE CIRCUS MAXIMUS,	Facing page 62
ADVANCING TO BATTLE,	70
NAPOLEON BONAPARTE,	75
SERPENT IN THE GLASS,	83
HANNIBAL'S VOW,	85
SUNRISE AT DOTHAN,	Facing page 88
THE OUTLOOK,	94
JOHN WESLEY,	102
OLIVER CROMWELL,	104
GENERAL GRANT,	107
PERFECT THROUGH SUFFERING,	Facing page 112
THE UNNOTICED VISITOR,	118
DAVID LIVINGSTONE,	126
AT THE FRONT,	129

	PAGE.
THE IRON DUKE,	136
THE BATTLE OF HASTINGS, ... Facing page	138
A NOBLE DRUMMER-BOY,	145
THE TRIAL,	148
THE TRIUMPH,	149
GREEK WARRIOR,	158
SWORD AND BIBLE,	165
QUEEN VICTORIA,	167
READY FOR ACTION,	169
A KNIGHT OF THE CROSS, ... Facing page	170
PIZARRO,	184
A WRECK,	189
LUTHER AT FOURTEEN,	194
ABRAHAM LINCOLN,	201
THE VISION OF CONSTANTINE, ... Facing page	204
THE SOLDIER AT HOME,	226
THE ARK,	228
LOOKING FORWARD,	232

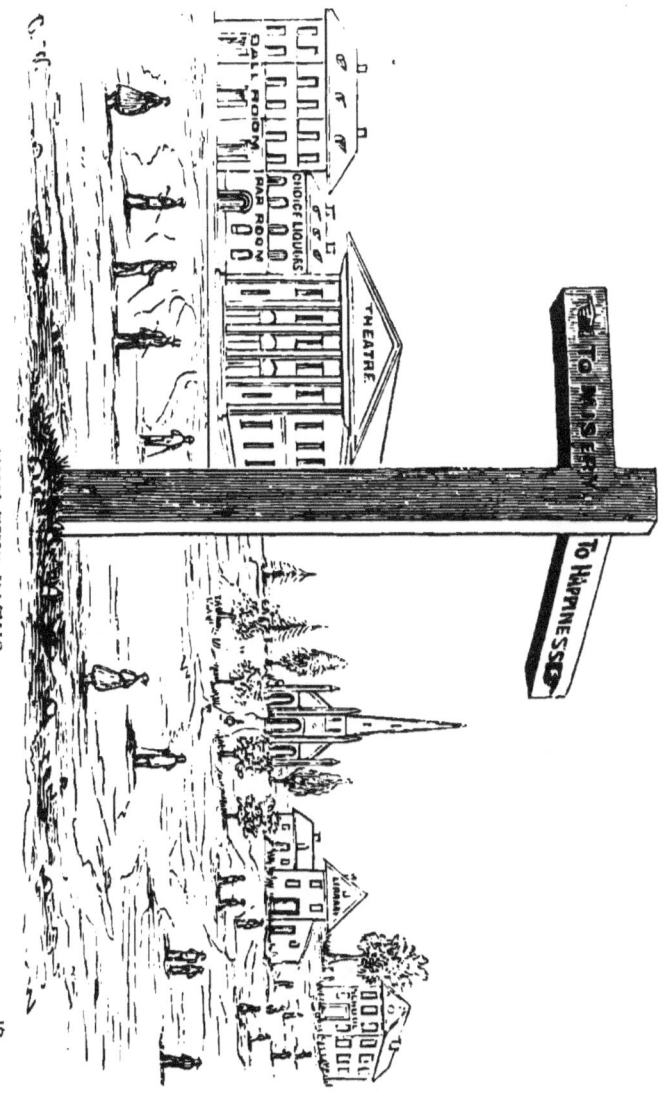

THE TWO PATHS

I.

CHOOSING SIDES.

CONTENTS.

INTERESTING SITUATION OF AN ANCIENT PEOPLE—WHAT IT MEANS TO LIVE—THE PERIOD OF MORAL HELPLESSNESS — HUMAN INCAPACITY COVERED BY DIVINE MERCY—STARTING OUT FOR OURSELVES—THE CHOOSING AND FORMATIVE PERIOD—SELF-MADE MEN NOT EXCEPTIONAL—DOES OPPORTUNITY MAKE THE MAN?—THE CHISEL OF DESTINY—THE GREATEST THING ON EARTH—WHY LIFE IS A BATTLE—MORAL NEUTRALITY NOT POSSIBLE—CHOICE LIMITED TO TWO SIDES—HOW TWO GREAT ARMIES ARE RECRUITED—LIFE'S DANGEROUS UNDERTOW—IMPORTANCE OF TURNING THE SWITCH—DRIFTING TOWARD THE RAPIDS—NECESSITY OF A FIXED AND WORTHY AIM—THE PROPER TIME TO ENLIST—IMPORTANCE OF RIGHT BEGINNINGS—OF TWO COURSES, WHICH?—GOD'S SERVICE A REASONABLE ONE—URGENT CALL TO DECISION—AN ULTIMATUM FROM HEAD-QUARTERS—TRUE MOTIVES OF A WORTHY LIFE.

I.
CHOOSING SIDES.

THE last shall be first. We draw our opening appeal from Joshua's final words to the Israelites. Like Washington, at a similar crisis, the chief concern of this ancient commander was that his countrymen should ever remember and ever illustrate the great truth that the only possible road to national exaltation was the broad highway of national righteousness.

These Israelites had been settled recently in a new land. Egypt, with its awful bondage, was behind them. Safely delivered were they also from the perils and the tedious marches of the wilderness. What had been so long only a promise, and sometimes, to their clouded vision, only a dim promise, was now a reality. Hope deferred had found its fruition. They were in Canaan.

Occupancy of this new land entailed new responsibilities, and of these their departing leader does not fail to remind them. Much had he to say, and every word, coming from such a source, must have been to these people like an apple of gold in a picture of silver. Summarized, however, the duty he urged was that, simply, of prompt and firm decision in favor of God—an intelligent and whole-hearted choice of the service of God—the precise duty which, beyond all others and before all others, presses upon all young people.

<small>Interesting Situation of an Ancient People.</small>

That which makes your duty the same as theirs, is the fact that your situation is similar. Had they entered Canaan but recently? So have you come recently within the sphere of moral obligation. You have been living for years; but now, as never before, do you begin to realize what it means to live. The tutelage and discipline of youth have led you at length to that momentous period in which responsibility presses, and opportunity

<small>What It Means to Live.</small>

invites, and temptations assail, just as these Israelites, after their training in the Wilderness, were settled at length as a separate and responsible people in the land of Canaan. Upon you, therefore, as upon them, does there rest now, with extraordinary force, the great duty of religious decision, that to which Joshua summons us when he says: "Choose you this day whom ye will serve."

In the earlier part of our existence the task of

The Period of Moral Helplessness.

choosing does not trouble us much. At that period others choose for us. They choose where we shall dwell, what we shall learn, what we shall be, what we shall do. And most fortunate is it that such an

JOSHUA.

arrangement exists; for of all animals man is the most helpless at his birth and for a number of years afterwards. Not only are we physically helpless at this period, but we are morally so as well. Not morally dead, for all children have some virtuous inclinations and some power of conscience. We affirm simply that we are morally incapable, during this period, of making a firm and intelligent choice of the course in life which would be best for us.

Happily, too, has our moral, no less than our physical, helplessness been provided for in the divine economy. Our fellow-beings choose for us in other matters, and, within this realm, until we are able to choose for ourselves, God chooses for us. He chooses, too, that we shall be his children, with his redemptive love as our portion while we live, and his own presence and glory if we die.

Human Incapacity Covered by Divine Mercy.

Later, however, as the will strengthens, as conscience develops, as the judgment becomes enlightened, and as the moral perceptions widen in their scope, our Heavenly Father severs these moral leading-strings, and sends us adrift, like an outgoing

Starting Out for Ourselves.

ship, which is towed by a tug while it is in the shallows near the shore, but which, when the shoals have been passed and the great stretch of old ocean rises to view, is left to carve out its own course, and to make what progress it can by the use of its own powers of locomotion.

At this momentous crisis are all those whom we distinctively call young people. As regards both your temporal and your spirit- *The Choosing and Formative Period.* ual destiny, this, pre-eminently, is your choosing period. Be assured, too, that within both realms your own individual choice is that which will determine what you are to be.

We hear men spoken of occasionally as "self-made men," and such cases are emphasized as though they were exceptional. *Self-made Men not Exceptional.* Let me tell you, however, that, in a very important sense, all men and all women are self-made. Parents may help to make us by the educational advantages they provide. But who could hold that education makes the man, in presence of the fact that so many who are educated fail in life, while some who are not educated, or are only partially educated, win for themselves a magnificent success.

Something may also be done toward making us by the openings which a kind Providence affords. But, spite of the fact that some one has had the temerity to say it, who can seriously believe that "opportunity makes the man," when we all know that many who are born to great opportunities barter their birthright for a mess of pottage, and that many others, who have only the advantages which they carve out for themselves by hard blows, reach the highest places of usefulness and honor?

Does Opportunity Make the Man?

Nor is the question of what we shall become determined by our mental endowments; for, as the slow tortoise, by keeping at it, will often outstrip the fleet-footed hare, so, in many cases, do those of moderate intellectual powers outstrip the more gifted in the race of life.

No, my young friends, none of these make the man, though each, if properly used, should contribute to this process. But that which really makes us—the sharp-edged and all-potent chisel by which every man, out of the block of marble that is placed before him, brings forth the angel or the demon—is

The Chisel of Destiny.

that man's own will. Greater this than all learning; greater than all the advantages of birth; mightier than brains; more potent, in one sense, than even the grace of God; for divine grace is never forced upon us, but is bestowed only where the will is used in seeking it. In other words, that which determines character and fixes destiny, is this stupendous prerogative of personal choice.

You talk about the power of kings; but let me tell you that the most absolute monarch on this earth is the king within your own breasts. Not only does the *The Greatest Thing on Earth.* Almighty himself respect the sovereignty of the will, but he has so arranged matters that all his creatures are compelled to defer to it. Were it possible, our parents, in most cases, would see that we turned out well. But in all the father's counsels that ever fell in golden nuggets from devoted lips, and in all the mother's tears that ever dampened a sleepless pillow or fell in scalding drops upon the cold cheek of youthful obduracy, there is not force enough to save a single soul from death, nor to turn the steps of one perverse mortal into the way of honor and renown. Thus we are all self-made men at last, and that which makes us what we are is

TAKING GOOD AIM.

this sublime, this inviolable prerogative of personal choice. To every one of us in early life comes the appeal to choose.

We present life to you as a battle, and the figure is aptly used. It is a battle; God has made it so. The mixture of good and evil in our own natures makes life a battle. The clash of opposing forces all about us makes it a battle. The din of conflict fills this whole universe. All intelligences are engaged. The Almighty wars against Satan, and Satan wars against God. On opposite sides are massed the good and bad angels. The great principle of wrong constantly antagonizes the mightier principle of right. *Why Life is a Battle.*

These aspects of the conflict we do not see; they are spiritual and invisible. But enough of this tug of war we do see to make the battle intensely real, and the necessity for taking part in it both clear and urgent. As regards the fact last named, it is as when, a generation ago, the crisis of war sent a line of division through this great Republic. Everybody then took sides. The heart in every case went one way or the other. Those who seemed to be neutral were not so in reality, and some of these had a harder time, with less to compensate them, than those who stood up *Moral Neutrality not Possible.*

boldly for their convictions. So in the battle of life. Our first duty, upon entering the arena, is to determine which side we will espouse.

That each must serve on one side or the other, is beyond question. Not only must the heart in-cline toward one or other of these two sides, but to one or the other will the service of the life be given. Here the analogy between the war for the Union and the conflict of which we are now speaking is lost. In our great National conflict thousands gave sympathy who did not don the uniform. But here, in every case, is service rendered; necessarily so, for this conflict is not confined to a few localities; it is raging constantly all about us, and, whether he will or not, every man has a part in it.

Choice Limited to Two Sides.

Not only must we all take sides in this battle, but all who would be upon the right side must enlist. The government of heaven, let us remind you, never resorts to the draft. It holds out inducements; it offers large bounty; it promises ample rations, splendid pay, a complete equipment, and it sends everywhere its recruiting officers, whose special business is to persuade men to enter the

How Two Great Armies are Recruited.

ranks. But beyond this God does not go. All his soldiers must be volunteers. He never has recourse to the draft.

With Satan, however, it is different. The draft is his normal process, and that upon which he mainly relies to keep up his forces. Only the few, only the most depraved and hardened, enter Satan's service from choice, the simple reason why he has so large a following being that all who refuse to enter God's army ally themselves with him of necessity; for so tightly in all directions are the lines of moral combat drawn, that he who is not with God is against him, and that he who enlists not of his own free will under the banner of moral progress, places himself, by his indecision, on the other side in this great conflict.

The undertow of life is toward evil and ruin. To lose the good and secure the evil, you need only neglect to choose the good. The sad wail of all lost souls, and <small>Life's Dangerous Undertow.</small> of all ruined lives is like the never-ceasing lament of that man who lost his reason because one night, as the express came dashing along, he neglected to turn the switch, and thus allowed the train, with its living freight, to dash forward to an awful destruction, his bitter deprecation, until he died, being, "O that I had! O that I had!" Yes, it would indeed have been better had he done his duty, inestimably better; but he had not, and hence the frightful consequences.

So, my young friends, does everything, in your case, depend upon whether or not, at the right time, you turn, or fail to turn. the switch of that sovereign will with which God has endowed you; for to turn this from its inclination toward evil, so that it shall open the track of righteousness to your steps, will mean salvation for both worlds; whereas to neglect to turn it will be, without the need of any further choice on your part, to leave the express train of destiny with no alternative but to dash forward on the road in which all danger lies, and the end of which is present and eternal destruction.

The Importance of 'Turning the Switch.

We repeat, therefore, with added emphasis, that the undertow of life is toward evil. To go up stream, one must pull vigorously; to go down stream, all you need do is just fold your arms and let the boat take her own course.

A number of gentlemen started on a certain occasion to cross the broad river running past Thun, in Switzerland, and one of them relates that in the middle of the stream they became involved in a controversy as to the point toward which they should make on the opposite shore, and this discussion, he says, continued so long that, before they knew of their danger, the undertow had carried them so far toward the rapids that it was only by the most Herculean efforts that they were able to bring the boat back, and thus save their lives. *Drifting Toward the Rapids.*

And what a warning does this afford against the insidious undertow which ever surges 'neath the placid stream of life! O young people, let us plead with you to regard this warning! Instead of parleying or playing or trifling in any way, after your boat has been fairly launched upon this stream, the true course is, to pull, without delay and without cessation, for the shore on the opposite side. In other words, have an object in life. Fix your gaze upon a point of destination; let it be a worthy one—no other than the arms of Christ and the service of Almighty God; and then, *Necessity of a Fixed and Worthy Aim.*

your point of landing chosen, bend all your energies to the task of reaching it; for be assured that, unless you do this, the current of the stream will bear you upon its treacherous bosom to places below, where the landing will be more difficult, and may possibly carry you into the rapids, where hope of being able to disembark will be still further removed, and, these passed, may finally plunge you over the cataract, and thus add one more to the millions of misguided souls who, because they did not choose to serve God, have been drafted into Satan's service, and, because they would not come to Christ for life, have been carried forward, of necessity, by the force of their own passions in the way which leads to death.

From these observations we shall surely be convinced, not only that it is our duty to enlist, but that it is our duty to do this immediately. This was the chief point in Joshua's appeal to the Israelites. Further delay, he felt, would be at once unreasonable, ungrateful, unwise, and unsafe. They could not doubt that it was their duty to serve the Lord, nor could they question in which direction

The Proper Time to Enlist.

STEERING BY THE CHART.

their own interests lay. The sad consequences of departing from the living God they knew well, from both observation and experience; and equally were they apprised of the blessedness which must result from being true to him. Obedient service, they were fully aware, meant life and prosperity; it meant national greatness and perpetuity. And just as fully did they know that disobedience meant national weakness, discomfiture, disintegration, and, if long persisted in, national destruction. They did not need any more light, nor could they reasonably ask for any additional discipline. They knew the way perfectly. Why should they hesitate another moment to walk in it? It was Joshua's conviction that these people were without excuse, not only for any further rebellion, but for any additional delay. Hence his fervent appeal to them to choose at once whom they would serve.

He must have felt also that an immediate decision was called for by the peculiar situation in which they were placed. Brought by the good hand of God into a new country, and newly invested as they were with national responsibility, what more fitting than

<small>Importance of Right Beginnings.</small>

that they should at once acknowledge God as their king, and begin immediately to serve him? An important epoch was this; it was the beginning of a new era, and Joshua, well knowing how much the beginning has to do with the continuance and the ending, did all he could, in his closing address, to prevail upon these Israelites to begin their new life in that new country by choosing to serve—to fully serve and to constantly serve—him whose right hand and outstretched arm had delivered them from the bondage of Egypt. These were the grounds of Joshua's urgency in the appeal he made to the Jews, and upon similar grounds do we base the appeal we are making to these young people.

Like the Israelites, you are just now in a new land. The novelty and the blessedness are yours of having recently entered the teeming realm of moral accountability.

Of Two Courses, Which?

Of all times, this is the time to begin a new life. Delay in serving God means the giving of your best powers and your best years to Satan's service. Moreover, if you do not enlist now, and do enlist later, you will have to change sides in life's conflict. But how much better to begin right than to get right afterwards! How much nobler to serve God from the first, than to serve the world first, and then offer to the Almighty the mere remnants of a life wasted and dishonored by sin!

Duty summons to the former of these courses. Remember, my young friends, that you are not your own, but that, by creative right and by redemptive purchase, you belong to God. *God's Service a Reasonable One.* Bear in mind, too, that the service he asks from you is a reasonable service; not impossibilities, but only the best you can do; not sacrifices without recompense, but a fullness of reward which shall more than make up for everything you lose, and shall fully repay you for any exertion you may make.

And every consideration which renders it necessary or desirable that you should serve God at any time, makes it both necessary and desirable that you should enlist *Urgent Call to Decision.* in his service without delay; for if you are his, it is beyond a question that you owe him, not a part of your life only, but the whole of it. And if, again, God's service be, as you admit, a reasonable service, then, we ask, how can any reasonable being justify himself in holding aloof from it for even a day?

Thus we draw a circle about you, and we ask you to choose whom you will serve ere you step beyond the limits of that circle. We come to you, as the ambassador of the Roman Senate went to Antiochus, in Egypt, with urgent commands to him to withdraw his armies from that country; and as he did, so do we; that is, we draw, as has been said, an imaginary circle about you, and call upon you to decide, here and now, whom you will serve. Possibly it would be at once truer and more impressive to say that the hand of God has drawn such a circle about you, and that from him really comes this appeal for an immediate decision. This circle is the mystic line inclosing that most momentous period of life between accountability and manhood. Some of you are standing in that charmed circle at this moment. God has placed you there. And now—your past lives filled with tokens of his goodness, and your future career brightend by promises of his continued favor—he stands before you, as Joshua stood before Israel, and the appeal he makes,

[margin: An Ultimatum from Head-quarters.]

the command he gives, is, "Choose you this day whom ye will serve."

We do not say that those who fail to choose in youth will never choose; nor do we affirm that by not choosing at once you of necessity run any great risk. *The True Motives of a Worthy Life.* Our hope is that you may have many opportunities of salvation. Probably you will, though, on the other hand, is the possibility that you may not. Still, we do not desire, and do not expect, to frighten you into decision. Our appeal is not to your fears, but to motives and impulses that are praiseworthy and noble.

Young people pride themselves in their sense of honor. O that this delicate sense of what is honorable and right might impel you all to do that which is right toward the God who made you and the Christ by whom you have been redeemed!

Young people are ambitious; they have exalted notions of what they would like to accomplish in life. Come, then, my young friends, and find the full realization of your highest and grandest dreams in this army of the Lord of hosts.

Young people are valiant; the glow of enthusiasm is upon them, and the tide of life flows buoyantly through their veins. "I write unto you, young men, because ye are strong," John said; and for the same reason do we write; and what we ask of you is that you make a consecration of this youthful strength, with all the valor and all the enthusiasm attending it, to the Being from whom it came, that gracious Being whose heart pulsates in tender love toward all his creatures—particularly toward all young people—and all of whose limitless resources are pledged in this battle of life to the overthrow of the powers of evil, and to the final vindication and triumph of every soldier who fights under his banner.

THE FLAG WE FOLLOW.

II.

THE FLAG WE FOLLOW.

CONTENTS.

An Ancient Battle-hymn—A Sweet Singer and his Chief Musician—How Battle-hymns stimulate to Valor—Times which try the Soul—Victory only by doing Duty—Use of Flags at Sea—Some who carry Satan's Flag—Two Flags which never harmonize—The Eloquence of Flags—Principles represented by the Flag we follow—A Flag which stands for Honesty, Purity, and Benevolence—The Standard of Moral Progress—The American Flag in 1812—How the Flag we follow has extended its Conquests—A Flag with a Mighty Future—Destiny of the Dark Continent—The American Flag in Siberia—What it means to have Heaven's Flag above us—His Satanic Majesty and the Czar of Russia—A Flag which symbolizes Hope and Help for All—What we owe to the Flag we follow—"Do n't let that Flag go down"—One who died for the Flag—Advantages of keeping our Colors Flying.

II.
THE FLAG WE FOLLOW.

HERE is an intimate relation between battle-flags and battle-hymns. It is from the former that the latter derive their inspiration. Often, too, the magic power of these hymns is concentrated in some distinct allusion to what the flag represents. This was the case with that battle-hymn of Israel which is preserved in the twentieth Psalm, one of the verses of which reads: " We will rejoice in thy salvation, and in the name of our God will we set up our banners."

In all probability this was Israel's favorite battle-hymn. It was penned by their warrior king, the valiant David, and its lofty sentiments do equal credit

An Ancient Battle-hymn.

to his intelligence, his daring, and his sublime faith. What the tune was we do not know. We can imagine, however, that the music would be pitched, like the words, in the highest key of genius, and would scale, as they did, the loftiest summits of patriotic fervor.

Assurance of this is afforded by the title to the Psalm, which intimates not only that it was a Psalm of David, but that it was dedicated by David to the chief musician; accompanied, too, we may well suppose, with a command from its royal author that the chief musician do his best to provide a score that would be worthy of it.

A Sweet Singer and his Chief Musician.

What a history must this battle-hymn have had! How often had its notes echoed and re-echoed through the spacious courts of Israel's magnificent temple! It was used in the temple service responsively. The priests would first render a verse, and then from ten thousand voices, blended in thundering chorus, the answer would be given in the next verse. But to hear this hymn at its best, we must wait until war impends and the martial spirit is abroad; or, better still, until Israel's army is about to charge upon her enemies. Then let the soldiers sing it for us as they rush into battle.

Imagine the effect of such a hymn. If the shrill music of the *Marsellaise* has such power over the soldiers of France, and if "The Watch on the Rhine," has so often sent the stolid Germans to victory, what wonder that, going into battle with the music of this Psalm in their souls, the armies of Israel were so often victorious? The fact is, indeed, that to Israel's hosts, when this battle-hymn expressed their real sentiments, victory was a foregone conclusion, and defeat a contingency not to be dreamed of; for this hymn made the conflict upon which they entered no longer a battle of men against men simply, but a battle of God against men. Of this they were aware; and knowing that their victory was so fully assured, what more natural or proper than that, as the Psalmist causes them to do in the words we have quoted, they should rejoice in it beforehand, and especially so since he supplied in the same sentence a fitting recognition of the Being by whose gracious power the victory was to be won?

Marginal note: How Battle-hymns Stimulate to Valor.

And now look at the application. Had they battles to fight? So have you. Your whole life will be a battle. The struggle against evil will be a never-ceasing one; and, in addition to this, there will be times when special conflict will impend—times which will try your souls as Hezekiah's was tried when the king of Assyria threatened him with destruction—conflicts which will shape character and fix destiny, as the character and destiny of Jacob were fixed by that long, lone, and finally victorious struggle with the angel. But let not our young friends be alarmed at this prospect; for what though life be a battle, if victory is assured beforehand? What though, as Israel was, you are beset by enemies, when you also have Israel's God to help and deliver you?

Times Which Try the Soul.

Do not forget, however, that in your case, as in theirs, deliverance is conditioned upon conduct. The salvation itself is from God, but the means which make it available inhere in your own hearts. If, therefore, you would exult in the victory which is promised, be sure that you perform the

Victory Only by Doing Duty.

duty imposed; be sure, that is, that at the very outset of life, as well as in preparing for every subsequent conflict, you set up your banners in the name of God.

Here, then, is the flag we follow—a flag raised in the name of God; a flag which, as we lift it up, and as the breezes of heaven unfold it to the gaze of mankind, shall unmistakably proclaim, first, that we are upon God's side; and, secondly, that God is upon our side.

The first thing is to raise this flag. The first duty is to choose sides. Don't imagine that you can be neutral. Out at sea, vessels recognize one another by the flags they display. <small>Use of Flags at Sea.</small> There is a language of flags. By these signs they tell each other who they are, whither they are bound, what cargo they carry, what weather they have met, and how it fares with those on board. Sometimes, though, a vessel will come within hailing distance of another without speaking. Not a solitary flag is raised; and, of course, when this occurs, the information the flags would so easily have given is left to conjecture.

But human beings are different from ships. From the mast-head of every bark navigating the ocean of human life some flag may be seen flying; and that flag proclaims who we are, whose allegiance we own, and whither we are bound. Which flag, we wonder, are these young people carrying? If it be the flag of worldliness, or the flag of indifference, or the flag of profanity, or the flag of intemperance, or the flag of dishonesty, or the flag of indecision, then it is the devil's flag; and the banner floating over you proclaims you to belong to him, and to be sailing under his guidance, through hidden rocks of danger, toward the port of final destruction. But we beg you to strike this flag, and to run up in its place the ensign of truth and righteousness.

Some Who Carry the Devil's Flag.

Sometimes, in naval battles, when one ship conquers another, the flag of the conqueror is hoisted above that of the vanquished, and the two float from the same mast-head together. But we do not like this arrangement. It is too suggestive of the position of compromise which some men and women are trying to maintain in the battle of

Two Flags Which Never Harmonize.

life. Rest assured, though, that to serve God and mammon at one and the same time is not possible. Rest assured, my young friends, that God's flag and the devil's flag never float together over the same individual, even though there may be an effort to give God's flag the pre-eminence. Hence we do not ask for a choice at your hands which shall merely put God's flag above that of Satan; but what we do ask, what we insist upon, and that which God imperatively demands, is that you take the old flag down and burn it, and that then, in token of a complete surrender, you run up in its place this new flag, which shall proclaim unmistakably that you have entered the Lord's service, and are voyaging now, under his skillful pilotage, not toward danger, but toward security; not to the port of final destruction, but to the safe harbor of eternal blessedness.

Every flag has its significance, and every flag representing a nation or a cause makes some kind of an appeal. Allusion has been made to the language of flags. *The Eloquence of Flags.* Think of the eloquence of these silent symbols, the power they have to stir the feelings, to set the soul on fire, and to waken into quenchless ardor the sleeping energies of the life! There have been times when the greatest orators, in appearing before an audience, have not needed to speak; when words would have been too barren and beggarly; when all they have done, or have needed to do, was to wave before the people some flag that was near by, the tumult following this act being such as old Boreas creates when, by his mighty winds, he lashes the ocean into a fury, and sweeps everything before him. There are times, too, when nothing so surely as a flag will awaken the softer feelings which, like swollen rain-clouds, vent themselves in tears. A tattered battle-flag, for instance,—what veteran and what patriot can look upon such an emblem, remembering what it means, without yielding to it an involuntary tribute of emotion?

Speaking, however, of the power which flags have to send a thrill through human hearts, and to throw a charm over human lives, what shall be said of this flag, this banner which is set up in the name of God, this blood-stained banner of the cross?

Consider, first, the principles it represents. They are principles of righteousness; for wherever this flag receives due reverence men will love justice and practice truth.

<small>Principles Represented by the Flag we Follow.</small>

"God and my right," is the motto on England's flag. Sometimes, though, that nation seeks more than her right. There are occasions when she infringes upon the rights of others.

But this flag of ours means "God and my right" in the truest and broadest sense; for it means not only that we shall do right so far as our own interests are concerned, but that we shall respect and promote the rights and interests of our fellow-creatures.

This flag stands for honesty. Let it be everywhere regarded, and we should need no longer either police-officers or prisons. It means purity. Let it float over our cities and exercise its virtuous sway over our lives, and personal chastity would everywhere prevail, doing away at once with divorce courts and with the dens of vice which abound amongst us. It means benevolence. Measure for us the length and breadth of God's benevolence, and we will then compute for you the length and the breadth, the strength and the beauty of those principles of benevolence symbolized by the banner which is lifted up in his name. Tell us what he is to his creatures, and we will tell you from that what this flag signifies to them.

<small>A Flag which Stands for Honesty, Purity, and Benevolence.</small>

It means liberty and temperance. Let us lift it up as individuals, and it will typify a redeemed manhood, a character made beautiful with the beauty of holiness, and a life which shall exhale goodness as naturally as the rose emits fragrance. Run up this flag over your dwelling, and it will mean that the earthly home has become typical of the heavenly. Hoist it from your city buildings, and it will proclaim that city officials have ceased to seek primarily their own good, and are seeking first the good of the community.

<small>The Flag of Moral Progress.</small>

Float it out upon the breezes from our State capitols, and let it open its white folds to the kisses of the sunbeams as they fall upon that great dome at Washington, and it will mean that the States which compose this Union shall be as sisterly and loving as the Three Graces, and our Nation the purest, the noblest, and the most enduring that God's blessed sun ever looked down upon. Such are some of the principles represented by this flag, such some of the gracious results that would ensue to human beings and to human society if all should follow this flag.

Look, too, at the halo of glory which encircles this emblem. It could not be other than a glorious flag, owing to the grandeur and glory of the principles it represents. It is glorious, too, because of the triumphs it has won. Like the flag of our own Republic, only in a higher and fuller sense, it has constantly increased in glory. The time was when our National ensign was not much esteemed; when, in fact, some nations held it in contempt. It is said that the British newspapers in 1812 expressed amazement and disgust,

The American Flag in 1812.

because, as they put it, the time-honored flag of England had been disgraced by "a piece of striped bunting flying at the mast-head of a few fir-built frigates manned by a handful of outlaws." Nor is this surprising, for in that year, we are told, two hundred and fifty British ships, carrying three thousand sailors, and cargoes of immense value, had been captured by American cruisers. No wonder the English were disgusted. But that piece of despised bunting, backed by the arms and hearts of free American citizens, did its business sufficiently well even at that time, though what it meant then, and what it did then, were but the faintest prophecies of the strength and glory for which it stands to-day.

So, and much more so, with this flag of the lowly Nazarene. The powers of the world held it in contempt at first. It was in their view only a piece of striped bunting, with a few outlaws behind it. But it answered all purposes even then; for at the very time when it was most despised, it began the winning of its greatest victories. While men were still spitting upon it, it was hoisted over the palace of the Cæsars;

How the Flag we Follow has Extended its Conquests.

and so, ever since, has it gone forward from victory unto victory, until now there is not a civilized power in the world that does not bow to it, and scarcely a foot of land on the earth where it may not be freely lifted up; or, recurring to our original figure, not a ship navigating the great ocean of modern progress which does not give this gospel ship the right of way, and which does not hasten to salute the glorious flag it carries.

Think, too, of the future that is before this flag. Think of the mighty plans of conquest for which it stands. How insignificant, in comparison to these, are the petty ambitions represented by other flags! The flag of these United States, they say, is destined to float finally over a united American continent. But God claims all the continents, and some day he will unquestionably get them. Russia is jealously watched by her European neighbors, because of the designs she has upon the Black Sea and upon Constantinople. But God has designs upon all the seas and upon all the cities and empires. A point of attraction for all the nations just now is the Dark Continent. It appears to be the destiny of that

A Flag with a Mighty Future.

land to be divided piecemeal among the European powers. Germany, England, France, Belgium, Portugal, all want a slice of it, with others yet to hear from.

Let me tell you, though, that Africa, like the other continents of this globe, has been pre-empted by the Government of heaven. Let me remind you that amongst the other flags planted in her fertile soil, is this flag of the Nazarene, and that, if prophecy be true and the current of events be a reliable criterion, this flag is destined to extend its triumphs there until Ethiopia shall stretch out her hands to God, and every corner of that Dark Continent be filled with the glory of his salvation.

<small>Destiny of the Dark Continent.</small>

This, my young friends, is the flag we follow—the best, the grandest flag that ever spread its folds to the free breezes of the sky—a flag which stands not only for universal conquest, but for universal and eternal dominion, according to the principles of righteousness.

As a still further inducement to follow this flag, think now of the power it symbolizes and the ample protection it insures.

THE FLAG WE FOLLOW. 55

Once enlist under this standard, and all the moral power of the Government of God is behind you. *The American Flag in Siberia.* How much it means sometimes to be a citizen of the United States! We have just had an illustration of this. A subject of the czar of Russia became a naturalized citizen of this country, and then, returning to his own country on a visit, he was seized and banished to Siberia, upon the pretext that he had fled to America to escape military service. Think of that man, exiled in that barbarous land, and with all the power of that great Government employed to keep him there! He is there, however, no longer. He is now back again in the land of his adoption. What accomplished all this? do you ask. Why, the American flag accomplished it by the power it has and the determination it shows to defend the rights and to guard the liberties of all American citizens.

But if it means something, and means so much, to be a citizen of this Government, and to have the American flag behind us, how much more must it mean to be a citizen of heaven's Government, and to have our moral and spiritual rights linked to the power, and bound up in the honor, of the flag which floats from the battlements of the skies!

What it Means to have Heaven's Flag Behind us.

In one respect there is a striking similarity between the Government of the czar of Russia and that control over mankind which Satan is seeking. We refer, of course, to the purpose of the latter to force as many as he possibly can into active service in his army. Not only will he use all his power to prevent you from enlisting in God's army in the first instance, but he will do all he can, in case you do enlist, to take you captive after-

His Satanic Majesty and the Czar of Russia.

wards. Let me tell you, too, that Siberia, with all its horrors, is an Eden of blessedness compared to the prison in which Satan immures his captives. But let me tell you this as well, that, malignant as are his designs, stupendous as is his power, and innumerable as are his emissaries, you still, if true to your colors as a soldier of King Jesus, need have no more fear of being harmed by him than though he had no existence.

But suppose, in an evil moment, we yield to Satan, what then? some one is asking. Why, then, do not think of despairing, but remember that this flag which we offer, if you shall but grasp it in the firm hand of faith, will work deliverance for you even in that case; for as there was no prison in Siberia strong enough, nor sufficiently remote, to conceal an American citizen from the vigilance of the American Government, or to detain him against the power of the American flag, so is there no corner in all the desert wastes of sin where any true penitent can be concealed from the Divine eye, or held for a moment in Satan's bondage against the power of divine grace. *A Flag which Symbolizes Hope and Help for All.*

And now, what does not such a flag deserve

from us? What of consecration, what of sacrifice, what of affection, what of devotion, what of service and fealty, can we reasonably withhold in presence of a standard so pure, so noble, so mighty, so divine? When Julius Cæsar, having crossed the Rubicon, in his march toward Rome, was informed that the senators had fled without striking a blow, he exclaimed in derision, as well he might: "If they will not fight for such a city, what city will they fight for?" So, of these young people, might it well be said, though we do not say it in derision, but in compassion and with tender yearning, if they will not fight in such a cause, and under such a flag as that which is here presented, in what cause will they fight, and to what flag, actual or conceivable, can we have any hope of gaining their allegiance?

What we Owe to the Flag we Follow.

JULIUS CÆSAR.

But many are enlisted under this banner

and they feel, doubtless, that to follow such a flag is an unspeakable honor. Some probably have the spirit of that wounded soldier, to whom his country's flag was everything, and his own sufferings and sacrifices nothing. "Never mind me, Captain," he said, "but don't let that flag go down." He had been wounded; he must soon bleed to death. His captain, who was near, saw his danger, and would fain have helped him. But the brave soldier begged him to push on. His own life was nothing, if but his country might be saved. "Never mind me, Captain," he said, "but don't let that flag go down." O, for such a spirit in those Christian warriors who fight under the banner of King Immanuel, whose cause is the cause of God, whose country is the New Jerusalem, and the success of whose arms will mean blessing, not to one nation alone, but to all the nations of the earth! If for other flags men will suffer so much, what suffering should we begrudge in behalf of this flag? If other flags appeal with so much force to the affections of those who follow them, how may not God's soldiers be expected to love his banner?

"Don't let that Flag go Down."

Think of that Austrian officer, found by the victorious Prussians, dying in a ditch. It is said that the Prussians who found him told the story with uncovered heads. He was flat upon his back. Help might have saved him, but he begged them to let him alone. So fervently did he beseech them to let him die just as he was, that they regarded his wishes in the matter. Passing that way again, and perceiving that he was dead, they began to prepare him for burial, and as they lifted him for this purpose, they saw at once why it was he had begged them so earnestly to let him die just where he was; for beneath him, hidden from the view of its enemies, had lain a tattered battle-flag, which evidently had been dearer to him than his own life. O, noble spirit! No wonder those Prussians admired it; no wonder they looked upon this scene with uncovered heads. Nor are we surprised that they should show their sense of such devotion by wrapping his body in this cherished emblem, and by laying him away for his long and well-earned rest with the flag he loved so well serving as his shroud.

[Sidenote: One who Died for the Flag.]

And now, my young friends, we would have you love in the same way, and defend with the same zeal, and guard with the same devotion, this better flag which you are following. Be sure, first, that you enlist under this banner; then be sure that you remain faithful. Be true to your convictions, maintain a bold front, keep your colors flying. Let all who know you, know on which side you are, and let them always know that you are on God's side. *Advantages of Keeping our Colors Flying.* To have no flag up, will be to invite assault from pirates, whereas the sight of your flag will protect you from such assaults; just as it was, a few weeks ago, with one of our own ships. Being followed by a craft which seemed bent on mischief, the captain, as a measure of safety, floated the American flag from the mast-head, the result being that the vessel which had seemed to threaten harm, soon found that it had urgent business in another direction. And so, rest assured, will Satan take to flight when he sees our flag hoisted. The better course, however, is not to hoist this flag in emergencies only, but to keep it flying all the time.

It has been touchingly observed that when Commodore Smith heard that the *Congress*, commanded by his son, had struck her colors, his simple observation was: "Then Joe is dead." And Joe was dead, and that remark was a noble father's best eulogy upon a faithful son. Such a spirit of heroism, such a well-established reputation for fidelity, God grant that you may have! Then, your banners set up in God's name, and your life devoted to his cause, it shall indeed become your privilege to rejoice continually in God's salvation; for in that case he himself shall go before you, and his power and grace ever enable you to triumph.

IN THE CIRCUS MAXIMUS.

III.

THE FOES WE FIGHT.

CONTENTS.

THE GREAT OPPORTUNITY OF A GREAT MAN—HOW OPPOSITION SHOULD INCITE TO HEROISM—THE CIRCUS MAXIMUS AND ITS LESSONS—WHAT IT MEANS TO BE AT LIFE'S THRESHOLD—PRIZES OFFERED IN THE ARENA OF EXISTENCE—REPUTATION DETERMINED BY CHARACTER—HOW TO WIN A COMMANDING POSITION—A GRAND PRIZE WHICH IS POSSIBLE TO ALL—THE GREAT PRIZE AT THE END—VICTORY ONLY THROUGH BATTLE—OUR MIGHTIEST FOE, AND HIS METHODS OF ASSAULT—LESSON FROM THE GREAT BONAPARTE—A FIGHTING CHANCE TO WIN—WHY GENERAL LEE FAILED—HOW INDUSTRY DISCOUNTS GENIUS—THE MOST COMMON VICE, WHAT IS IT?—THAT INSIDIOUS FOE, DISHONESTY—THE TRUE WAY TO GET ON IN LIFE—AWFUL CONSEQUENCES OF IMPURITY—TENACITY OF YOUTHFUL HABITS—APPALLING EFFECTS OF INTEMPERANCE—PLEDGING THE MODERN HANNIBALS—HOW TO ACHIEVE THE MOST BRILLIANT CONQUESTS—BRIGHT SIDE OF THE BATTLE OF LIFE.

III.

THE FOES WE FIGHT.

TO be assailed by numerous foes, and to win their victory at last only by the most determined and persistent fighting, has been the invariable lot of earnest and virtuous souls since the world began. This was Paul's situation when, from Ephesus, he wrote to his friends in Corinth, saying: "A great door and effectual is opened to me, and there are many adversaries." Before him was an open door, and beyond that door was a broad sphere of Christian activity Not only a chance to work, but the certainty, if he should work, that unusual results would follow his labors; for this door, he tells us, was at once a a great and an effectual door. Thus the situation seemed enviable in the extreme, and the prospect all that could be desired. But with so much to encourage, was there nothing to dishearten?

We do not wonder at Paul's purpose to tarry indefinitely at Ephesus when we take only this view of his position. Perhaps, though, The Great Opportunity of a Great Man. there is another view. Possibly there are facts which, had they been fully realized, might have inclined the apostle to leave Ephesus. There was, indeed, another side to the situation, and a side, too, in the survey of which a less heroic soul than Paul's would unquestionably have been intimidated. There was opportunity; but there was opposition as well. There was an open door; but investing this door, to dispute his entrance therein, were many adversaries. And there were adversaries beyond the door, who would oppose his every effort, and contest desperately every foot of the progress he sought to make after the door had been passed. Bear in mind, too, that Paul knew this, and that in the passage we have quoted he makes distinct allusion to it; and yet observe, at the same time, in what spirit and with what terms he alludes to it.

Notice the conjunction employed. He does

not say, "A great door and effectual is opened to me," *but*, "there are many adversaries," as though the presence of these adversaries made duty uncertain and success dubious. What he does say, is, "A great door and effectual is opened to me, *and* there are many adversaries," as though these adversaries, far from furnishing a reason why he should leave his post in Ephesus, afforded the strongest reason why he should cling to it, making his presence and his continued labors in that city not only the more needful, so far as the cause of God was concerned, but the more desirable and the more honorable from the stand-point of his own personal interests. How Opposition should Incite to Heroism.

Such was Paul's view of the situation and prospects at Ephesus, and such is the view of life we would hold up before these young people. An open door means access to opportunities; a chance to do something and to be something; and the opening of a great door signifies that the chance presented is one of unusual magnitude and importance. Such is the chance you have.

This figure ot an open door beset by adversaries, is supposed to have been drawn by Paul from the opening of the great doors of the Circus Maximus, and from the opportunity thus afforded to win honor in the chariot-races. Assuming the correctness of this view, how strikingly suggestive does the passage become of the position occupied by these young people! Just now, my young friends, are there opened before your steps the great doors, not of the Circus Maximus, but of the mightier arena of human life We congratulate you, both upon the position you occupy and upon the prospects which are before you. To be at life's threshold, what a privilege! Would that you fully appreciated this privilege, and had a proper sense, also of the responsibilities attending it! But many, we fear, are deficient at this point, and hence our present effort to instruct them respecting it

The Circus Maximus and its Lessons.

As a means to this end, we would flash upon these opening doors of existence the lurid light of ten thousand hopeless death-beds. We would summon before you from the other side of those doors the ghosts of ten thousand wasted opportunities. We would also take you in thought over some of the battle-

What it Means to be at Life's Threshold.

fields lying beyond, and let you listen to the bitter wails of those who have been worsted in life's struggle, and at the same time we would remind you how many there have been who, because they entered life's battle with a just appreciation of what it meant, have carved out for themselves a magnificent triumph, winning the plaudits at once of earthly spectators and of those who watch this conflict from the battlements of the skies. These things we would do, if we could, to make you realize, as many, we fear, do not at present, how transcendently important is this open door of life, and how very necessary it is to your future success that you enter this door with proper feelings and with worthy purposes.

Look, first, at some of the prizes offered in life's arena. Some win the inestimable prize of a good character. They pre- *Prizes Offered in the Arena of* serve their integrity. They walk *Existence.* ever in that brightest of earthly pathways, the path made sunny by an approving conscience. They keep on good terms with themselves, which, next to being in friendly relations with God, is the greatest good any of us could desire, and that which most surely conduces to happiness.

A good character is almost always attended by a good name; for the rule is that the man who does right, stands right before his fellowmen. He may be evil spoken of at times; but how is it possible for the breath of calumny to taint such a man, or for the mud of slander permanently to defile him? As soon might the baying of midnight curs disturb the serenity or dim the luster of the white-faced moon. Yes, there are multitudes, thank God, who win in life the priceless guerdon of a good name,—that which is better than great riches; that which inspires confidence, and

Reputation Determined by Character

constrains affection, and commands preferment, and makes the memory, when we are gone, sweet and grateful as the pouring forth of fragrant ointment.

Some, moreover, win positions of prominence and commanding influence. And let us emphasize the fact that these high places are won. They are not in- herited, excepting in the very rarest instances; nor do they come at the caprice of good luck. Life is not a lottery, though many delude themselves with the notion that it is. Every man in this country is the architect of his own fortune, the contriver and fashioner of his own fame. Prizes are these things, and if some receive them and others do not, the reason is usually, if not invariably, that the fortunate ones so demean themselves in life's conflict as to win these prizes, while the others, largely through their own faults and deficiencies, become losers in this fierce strife. *How to Win a Commanding Position.*

A prize which, fortunately, may be secured by every one of us, is the blessedness of doing good. Though we may not all become distinguished, we can all be useful. To do good in the world we need not be richly endowed in intellect, nor is it necessary for us to attain to exalted position. The stars of night have their uses, equally necessary and blessed with those served by the full-orbed king of day; and so may the smallest and least gifted life, no less surely than the most brilliant and distinguished, shed radiance, according to its ability, upon this darkened world, and so fulfill its mission as to be as much missed when it has gone out, as the stars are when impenetrable clouds enshroud them.

<small>A Grand Prize Which is Possible to All.</small>

Nor can we afford, at this point, to leave out of the account the life that is beyond. If it be a great and effectual door which opens to you at the beginning, what shall be said of that opening at the end, that door of exit from life's arena to which John refers when he says, "I looked, and behold, a door was opened in heaven?" Not to all will that door open, but to those who are victorious it will, beyond a question. Thus there is held out to youthful ambition,

<small>The Great Prize at the End.</small>

> An honored life, a peaceful end,
> And heaven to crown it all.

And who will not join us in the wish that this prize, no less than the others mentioned, may be the final and eternal inheritance of these young people, who are objects of such profound interest to us because they are sitting now within the portals of these sublime possibilities?

Now, as to the warfare we are to wage.

The kingdom of heaven suffereth violence. We shall certainly have to fight if we would win that prize; and no less certain is it that fighting will be necessary *Victory Only through Battle.* if we are to gain any of the other prizes held out to us. At the door of every Eden of earthly blessedness stands an armed sentinel, surely as an angel with a flaming sword was posted by Almighty God at the gate of the first Eden. Ere Jonathan and his armor-bearer could scale the garrison of the Philistines, they must pass between two rocks,—Bozez, which meant dirty, and Seneh, which meant thorny; and just so are there thorny and dangerous passways to be traversed ere these young people can take any of the garrisons of honor and glory which lie before them.

When the doors of the Circus Maximus were

thrown open, not only was there a sharp contest at the entrance, but every step of the course was sharply contested; and precisely similar will you find it to be in this mightier contest in the arena of life. A great and effectual door opened to Paul, and standing guard over this door, to dispute his entrance therein, were many adversaries. So in your case.

The adversaries in this battle will be at once numerous and desperate. At their head will be <small>Our Mightiest Foe, and his Methods of Assault.</small> the prince of fallen spirits. You will not see this leader of the opposing forces, but you will feel his influence, and, unless you are extremely careful, will fall a prey to his strategy. His usual course is to take advantage of our natural passions and inclinations. As some one has forcibly put it, this great adversary, like a smith at his forge, blows with the breath of temptation upon the coals of human desire, until they are sufficiently heated to melt the purposes of the will, and then, our will having yielded, he bends and fashions us as he pleases.

This struggle against evil never ceases. It is a hand-to-hand encounter, and it is a battle

NAPOLEON BONAPARTE.

to the death. When Napoleon had captured Saragossa he found, it is said, that the battle was renewed in every street, and was not finally won until the desperate defenders of that city had been met and defeated singly and individ-- ually. So in this battle of life. First the citadel must be carried. First, by the power of divine grace, ascendency must be given to virtue and right principles. First we must be converted. The door of life's opportunities before us, and many adversaries standing there to beat us back, our first duty is to put these adversaries to the sword; and the sword to employ in this holy assault is the sword of the Spirit, which is the Word of God.

Lesson from the Great Napoleon.

Then, the first battle won and an entrance effected, what then? Why, then, my young friends, far from having earned the right to rest on your laurels, you have simply carved out for yourselves, by the grace of God, a fighting chance to win other victories; for then, as at Saragossa, will the battle be renewed in every street and the enemy assail you from every house-top, the price of your continued liberty being continued vigilance, and the good things of this world, equally with the better things of the other world, becoming yours to possess and enjoy only when

Our Fighting Chance to Win Victories.

THE FOES WE FIGHT.   77

you shall have deserved and conquered them by courageous and successful fighting.

So much in general about the foes you have to fight. Now we enter into a few particulars which will prove, we trust, more practical and useful. To say that the battle of life will never cease, and that your chief foe will be Satan, is to afford little light and to hold out little encouragement. Were that all we could say, we should leave you perplexed rather than instructed, and fearful instead of confident. Fortunately, however, there are statements to be made which are more definite. Fortunately, we are not ignorant of Satan's devices. An inspired apostle declares that we are not, and he tells the truth; for, in the first place, we have the Bible to instruct us, and, added to this, we have the teeming pages of human experience to draw upon.

Let me remind you, my young friends, that though the battles to which you are advancing will be new to you, they are not new to mankind in the abstract; for beings just like yourselves have been fighting similar battles since the world began, one of the results being that we know thoroughly our enemy's plan of campaign. It has been held, by one of his biographers, that the reason General Lee failed in his campaign in Pennsylvania and Maryland, was that, by some accident, his plans fell into the possession of the general opposing him. We do not know as to this; but that the plans of the skillful general opposing us in this battle of life have fallen into our hands, is beyond question. And hence the great practical advantage of looking over the field before you enter it, and of pausing while still on the outside of the great door of life until there shall have passed before you, in panoramic view, the two sides of life,—the opportunities it affords, and the dangers it presents; the prizes to be won, of which you have already been informed; and the foes to be fought, particular information of whom it is our purpose to give you now.

Why General Lee Failed.

One of our foes is indolence. A battle is always a scene of activity; and if life be a battle, what save inglorious defeat can possibly await those who sit at ease? Within both the spiritual and the secular realms the prizes and rewards fall alone to industrious workers. Talk not of genius; for often,

How Industry Discounts Genius.

whilst genius pines in rags, mediocrity, backed by honest endeavor, clothes itself in purple, and carries everything before it. Really, as the best thinkers are agreed, there is no genius but hard work. Energetic toil, steadily continued, is the wonder-worker of this age. There is nothing like it, nothing that can take its place. Not only is it a sure road to success, but it is, generally speaking, the only road to that goal.

To yield to indolence will render us an easy prey to other vices. Let the enemy find us with our armor off and our weapons stacked, and we are his every time. And with all the more earnestness do we warn you against indolence, because we are sadly aware of the natural proneness of mankind to yield to this foe. That philosopher told the truth who declared the most common vice of the human family to be sloth. We beg you, therefore, to keep free from this vice. Rouse yourself to effort. If you must fall in this battle, do n't let the enemy carry you off while you are asleep, but show the spirit of that noble soldier who insisted upon going to the front, even when he was too ill to go, and who, when admonished

The Most Common Vice, What is it?

by his captain that he would die if he went, replied: "Let me go anyway; for if I must die, I want death to find me, not in the ambulance, but on the field."

Another foe is dishonesty. One of the most insidious of our enemies is this, because he <small>That Insidious Foe, Dishonesty.</small> offers us a short road to comfort and wealth. Be assured, however, that he lies in making these promises. He offers comfort, and gives wretchedness; and what though dishonest gains enrich us for a time in a worldly sense, think of the price we pay to get them, in the sacrifice of integrity, of a good conscience, and of all hope of those imperishable riches that are laid up in heaven. Think, too, how uncertain is our hold upon such gains. Think how soon they may leave us in penury, rendered additionally odious by disgrace. Think, too, how often in these days, thanks to a quickened public conscience and a better administration of law, dishonesty finds its fitting recognition in the striped uniform of the penitentiary.

In warning young people against this foe, we do not assume either that they are thieves or are inclined to become such; but that they will be tempted, as they advance in life, to do many things which will not bear the light of honest scrutiny, is inevitable, from the false ideas and principles which are abroad. It was remarked once by a public speaker that the youth of his country reminded him of the three degrees of comparison: First, they tried to get on; then they tried to get honor; then they tried to get honest. But let me admonish you, my young friends, that the true way to get on in life, and the only way to get honor in life, is to be honest from the first, and to remain so ever afterward, spite of all temptations to a contrary course. *[The True Way to get on in Life.]*

Another foe is impurity; and how many fall victims to it! Its first approaches are in evil thoughts; then evil feelings; then, as the Scripture says, "When lust hath conceived, it bringeth forth sin; and sin, when it is finished, bringeth forth death." Among all the commands given by the veteran Paul to the young soldier Timothy, the very greatest was that he gave when he said, "Keep thyself pure." Impurity will weaken the body; it will vitiate *[Awful Consequences of Impurity.]*

and enfeeble the mind; it will blast the character; it will enslave the life; it will damn the soul; it will make our memory a stench, and will start influences and passions in others which will remain to torture mankind, and to curse the world, even after our own career shall have found its fitting termination in rottenness and infamy.

Why do we speak so strongly upon this subject to the young, does some one ask? Because, *Tenacity of Youthful Habits.* my friends, youth, from the very vigor of animal life which it has, is peculiarly susceptible to temptation at this point; because, moreover, youth is the time when habits are formed; and because, as the youth is, the future life is likely to be; and because, furthermore, if our young friends shall only succeed in keeping themselves pure in their early manhood, the victory gained is almost certain to be of life-long duration; whereas, should they fail to win this victory at that period, the probabilities are they will never win it.

Let me warn you also against another foe, the dread foe of intemperance. You want to be happy; but all happiness will disappear where intemperance casts his burning glance, quickly as the dews of night before the fiery face of the summer sun. You want to be successful, but success is no more possible under the dominion of drink than it would be possible for a man, single-handed, to resist successfully the mighty sweep of Niagara. Visions of domestic bliss rise in entrancing beauty over the landscape of your lives; but domestic happiness is conditioned upon purity and devotion; and how can a man be pure while his system is inflamed by alcohol, or a woman find the proper incentives of womanly devotion when the man who swore to cherish her is a brute?

Appalling Effects of Intemperance.

Did you ever look upon a blighted household? Did you ever listen to the sad moanings of a broken heart? Did you ever gaze with tearful eyes upon the fragments of a life wrecked and ruined beyond all hope of redemption? Have you the least idea what such things mean? Let me tell you, then, that more households have been blighted, more hearts broken, and more lives hopelessly wrecked by this foe of intemperance, than by all other evils together. Only think that to the fell demands of this insatiate monster our own country pays an annual tribute of at least seventy thousand drunkards' graves!

So, my young friends, let us swear you—as the father of Hannibal swore him in his youth to eternal hatred of old Rome—so let us swear you to eternal and unrelenting hostility at once against the drink-habit and the drink-traffic; for be assured that the only safe attitude toward a foe whose approaches are so insidious, and whose clutches are so deadly, is to give him no quarter or toleration at any point, but to plant yourselves in this warfare, and to ever remain upon the firm

Swearing the Modern Hannibals.

ground—that twin-rock of sure resistance and inviolable security—abstinence for the individual and prohibition for the State.

Another foe is indecision. Alexander, when asked how he had conquered the world, replied that he had done it by not delaying. O, young friends, the world is before you, and you may conquer it! In a far better than the Alexandrian sense may you conquer the world. Satan also is before you, seeking your destruction, and you may conquer him. Before you, too, lifting up a brazen and stubborn front, are a thousand other foes, and you may conquer every one of these. How shall you do this, does some one ask? Why, as Alex-

HANNIBAL'S VOW.

How to Achieve the Most Brilliant Conquests.

ander did, by not delaying; by not delaying when the tide of opportunity comes in to take it at the flood; by not delaying, when the tempter appears, to say, "Get thee behind me, Satan;" by not delaying to say No when the world invites to forbidden pleasures, or when passion impels toward that which would be impure; by not delaying, when God calls, to say, like Samuel, "Speak, Lord, for thy servant heareth;" by not delaying,—that is the way to carve out a worthy career in life; above all, by not delaying to give your hearts to God, and to fit yourselves for this great battle of life by putting on the whole armor of God.

Before you is an open door. Beyond that door is the entire stretch of active life. What would not some give could they put themselves back just where you are? What is there that is worthy and grand which you may not realize, if you but set yourselves to seek it in the fear of God? And what though there are many adversaries? Far from disheartening you, this fact should nerve you to valor. A life with no hardships in it would ill befit such beings as we are. No struggle, no

<small>Bright Side of the Battle of Life.</small>

development; no battle, no triumph; no contest, no prizes; no cross, no crown!

Sitting, therefore, as we do, within the portals of a great and effectual door, and clearly perceiving, as we must, that this door leads to conflict, let us not repine over this fact; but rather let us rejoice in it, thanking God that we have the privilege at once of doing something and of daring something; and while thus exulting in the opportunities God has given us, let us get ready to improve them, by lifting up a standard in his own name, and by seeking to realize, as we advance upon our foes, that the best of all is, God is with us.

SUNRISE AT DOTHAN.

Fear not: for they that be with us are more than they that be with them.

IV.

THE ALLIES WHO HELP US.

CONTENTS.

An Inspiring Panorama—Anxious Question of a Trembling Youth—Wise Words from the Lips of Experience—First View of Life—What it Reveals—An Eye-opening Prayer—Allies in Life's Battle whom we can not see—Lesson from the Sad Fate of Maximilian—The Mighty Government that Backs us—Help from Angels, may we expect this?—The Great Question, How?—Celestial Forces on Terrestrial Battle-fields—Angelic Help not Adequate to Human Need—Our Chief Reliance in Life's Battle—Advantages of having God with us—Comparative Estimate of those for and against us—A Winning Battle-cry—What is necessary to put God on our Side—The Great Strategic Point in Life's Battle—A Memorable Campaign, what it teaches—After Conversion, what?—Earthly Alliances which offer Help—Why we need the Church—Sterling Advice of an Old Sea-captain—Lesson from the Johnstown Flood—Another View of Life's Golden Morning—Helps to Success in Life.
90

IV.
THE ALLIES WHO HELP US.

IT is day-break on a mountain-top, and the early light, as it spreads over the face of nature, falls upon the up-turned and hopeful features of one who is in the early morning of existence. This youth is the servant of the prophet Elisha, and one of the old commentators remarks that Elisha had taught him good habits by teaching him to rise early.

The panorama of opening day is beautiful under any circumstances and to any eyes. To one, however, through whose veins courses the blood of youthful vigor, and who is so very fortunate as to view it from a commanding eminence, the sight is more than beautiful,—it is magnificent, it is really inspiring. Truly enviable, therefore, was the

<small>An Inspiring Panorama.</small>

91

position of this young man in one sense, and had it only been possible for him, while he looked at the glowing heavens, to shut out from his vision all sublunary sights and duties, he might have stood there enraptured and entranced until Aurora's train of light had drawn the full-orbed sun into view.

Of necessity, though, he had looked downward, and in so doing had beheld a sight which <small>Anxious Question of a Trembling Youth.</small> sent a shudder through his frame; for at the foot of the mountain was a warlike host, massed there, as his fears correctly informed him, with special designs against himself and his master. We do not wonder that under these circumstances the young man trembled, nor that his agitated feelings found vent in the question, "Alas! my master, what shall we do?"

But listen now to Elisha's answer. Older is the prophet than the servant and better informed. He has a longer stretch of experience <small>Wise Words from the Lips of Experience.</small> behind him. Not only has he seen the sun rise a larger number of times to gild the heavens with hope and glory, but more frequently to him, than to the boy who waits upon him, has the new day brought new perils; and invariably, too, in all these cases, have new dangers brought new opportunities for deliverance. His communings, moreover, were with the Divine. Behind the thin veil of nature he had found the God of nature. Such wonderful insight had he that he lived in two worlds at the same time, and saw as distinctly what was transpiring in the invisible as in the visible. His servant had seen that morning the breaking light of only one day; he had beheld at once a material and a spiritual sunrise. The youth's vision had taken in but the one army— that which had been massed for their destruction; the prophet's vision had compassed not only the earthly assailants, but the heavenly defenders, and the latter, presently, would his servant be made to see. Naturally, therefore, this man of God, far from being alarmed, is serenely peaceful and sublimely confident; his reply to the anxious question of his trembling companion being, "Fear not; for they that be with us are more than they that be with them."

Similarly situated to this servant of Elisha are those whom we are now addressing.

In the early morning of existence are they. Their vigorous feet tread firmly the mountain **First View of Life—What it Reveals.** heights of youth. It is sunrise with them. The horizon encompassed by their vision is tinted with rays of promise and lit up by the soft light of hope. O blessed eminence, from which youthful eyes

look out upon the opening prospect of life; and blessed sight the vision of daybreak which is there afforded! Equally, however, with the servant of Elisha, do these young people see, from the heights on which they stand, not only that which gladdens and inspires, but that which, in one view, is calculated to depress. They see enemies and the certainty of a great conflict before them; and hence the pressing need of this message of comfort and assurance. "Alas!" you ask, "how shall we do?" and our reply is, as Elisha's was: "Fear not; for they that be with us are more than they that be with them."

After addressing him in these words, Elisha prayed for this young man, his special supplication being that God would open his eyes, that he might see; and when his eyes were opened he did see, and what he saw was that, whereas he had supposed that Elisha and himself were alone, they were surrounded by all the forces of the skies, that the mountain on which they stood was full of horses and chariots of fire. *An Eye-opening Prayer.*

Would to God, my young friends, that your eyes might be opened, that you too might see how full of helpful forces is the mountain on which you stand! *Allies in Life's Battle whom we can not see.* Some of these can be apprehended, of course, only by the eye of faith. But they are no less real on that account, nor need the fact of their being invisible lessen in the least their potency for good. To the soldier on the battle-field the greatest helps are not those which he sees, but those which he feels without seeing. The Government, for instance, which sends him forth,—

he does not see this; he is far removed from it. But he relies upon it for his pay, he looks to it for his rewards, and he implicitly believes that, so far as it can, it will send re-enforcements to his help.

And let me tell you, my young friends, that there is a Government, and a mighty Government, at your back. Think not that the God who thrusts you into the battle will leave you to your own resources. If he did, he would be heartless beyond conception—more deserving of the reprobation of mankind than Napoleon III was held to be when he carried the hapless Maximilian to Mexico, and left him there, without protection, to the cruel mercies of a people whose throne he had usurped. This, however, God does not do. Far from it. He sends us to the battle-field at his own charges, and provides abundantly from his own resources for our vindication and triumph there.

Lesson from the Sad Fate of Maximilian.

Yes, there is a Government behind us in this battle of life, one upon which we can implicitly rely,—grander, mightier, and trustier than the best human Government this earth has ever known. We can not see it; but we are sure it exists, and that it helps us. Our consciousness attests this fact; for every faithful soldier in life's battle is supplied by this Government with a complete equipment and with ample pay, and is assured, moreover, by ten thousand promises, all of which have been tested and fulfilled in ten thousand times ten thousand instances, that he shall want for no good thing, and shall be brought off, finally, more than a conqueror. <small>The Mighty Government that Backs us.</small>

In Elisha's case this heavenly Government sent to the aid of its imperiled servant a large contingent of heavenly forces. May anything like this, you ask, be expected in the case of those who fight the battles of heaven at the present day? To which we reply, Why not? Our chief adversary being a fallen angel, what more reasonable than that amongst our helpers should be numbered the angels who have kept their first estate? If it be true, as the apostle says, that we wrestle not against flesh and blood, but against principalities and powers, and against wicked spirits in high places, it would seem as though the help <small>Help from Angels—May we Expect this?</small>

of good spirits were necessary to make the contest an evenly balanced one. And who can doubt, in the light of the New Testament, that these angels of God are indeed our allies? Does not Christ speak of the power he had to summon instantly twelve legions of angels? And assuming the angels to be divided into war-like legions, for what purpose can this be but to do battle for his cause and people? And, as though to make assurance doubly sure, does not Paul explicitly declare that all these angels are ministering spirits, sent forth to minister to those who shall be heirs of salvation?

In precisely what way these angels of God exert their influence in our behalf, we can not tell; nor would any good end be served by speculation upon this point. Suffice it to know, and to be assured, as we are, that they do exert an influence, that they do champion our cause, and, under the skillful generalship of the Captain of our salvation, are helping us in the battle of life.

The Great Question—How?

Thus does the opening light of existence reveal to you two hosts. Just as it was with the servant of Elisha that memorable morning at Dothan, and with Jacob when, at a great crisis in his life, the angels of God met him, and so impressed him by their presence that he called the name of the place Ma- <small>Celestial Forces on Terrestrial Battle-Fields.</small> hanaim, which means "two hosts,"—just as it was in these cases, precisely so is it in your case. The Government of heaven has not forgotten you; it does not leave you without sustenance, and will not leave you, in any time of need, without angelic re-enforcements. And if it was the proud boast of Pompey that by one stamp of his foot he could summon all Italy to arms, how much prouder, how much grander, how much more majestic and sublime, the privilege of these young people who, by the simple uplifting of an appeal to God, can summon all heaven to arms, and bring down to every mountain-top of terrestrial conflict the same celestial and invincible forces which were round about Elisha!

But these allies, powerful though they are, and helpful as their influence must necessarily be in life's battle, are neither our sole nor our chief reliance. Trust <small>Angelic Help not Adequate to Human Need.</small> alone in the angels, and you will lean upon a broken staff; for it is questionable if in the whole of God's universe there are enough of these intelligences to save a single soul, or to win for mankind, by their own unaided efforts, a single battle over either the world, the flesh, or the devil. Had any security been obtainable by committing our cause to angelic hands, our Father in heaven would no doubt have told us so. Yet in all his Word we are not advised in a single instance to trust in any of his creatures, not even in these brightest and best of all the intelligences he has brought into being. On the contrary, his constant instructions are that our confidence shall be stayed primarily and supremely upon himself.

Notice at this point the example of Elisha. He is not indifferent to the angels. He takes comfort from seeing them. He rejoices that they are with him. He is resolved, too, that his young servant shall see these celestial warriors. It is these, moreover, to whom he specially refers when he seeks to cheer this young man by telling him that they who are with them are more than those who are against them. Elisha's communings, however, were not with the angels, but with God. It was to God that he prayed;

it was upon God, and not upon any of the creatures of God, that his reliance was placed. Manifestly, too, was it from God that his deliverance and triumph came.

And this same Supreme Power, who was the supreme reliance of Elisha at Dothan, is the Being, beyond all others, upon whom these young people should rely in the battle of life. *Our Chief Reliance in Life's Battle.* We must have him with us, or the angels will not be with us, for they are his ministers, who do only his pleasure. We must have him to have them; and when we do have him, they come to our help of necessity; though if they did not, if for any reason our angelic allies failed us, and though, indeed, by some inconceivable mischance they were every one to sink out of existence, until in all the vast expanse above us not an angel's wing should stir, nor on all the avenues of heaven be heard again the rumbling of any of their fiery chariots,— even then, having God with us, we should be more than a match for all our foes, and more than victorious in every conflict.

The great Bonaparte was held to be himself equal to his entire army. His presence, that is, in the estimation of the opposite side, made the forces he commanded as strong again as they would have been without him. But O, my young friends, when God is on the field, he needs no forces. When he is near, the whole Government of heaven, and all the moral power in the universe, is at our back; for, as Paul triumphantly exclaims: "If God be for us, who can be against us!" As though all opposition were as insignificant in his presence as chaff in presence of the mighty wind, and as sure to vanish before his glance as the stars are to hide their diminished heads when the grand old sun heaves into view.

<small>Advantages of Having God with us.</small>

JOHN WESLEY.

Is it not true, therefore, that they who are with us are more than they who are with them? Counting the angels, and reckoning upon our side all the spirits of the just, and all the good people about us, there are more with us than against us,—far

<small>Comparative Estimate of Those for and Against us.</small>

more, even in the strict numerical sense; and, of course, if we weigh our forces, instead of counting them, all comparison is lost. If, however, you insist upon counting, then we beg you to hear God asking, How many do you count me?

The battle-cry of Cromwell's Ironsides was: "God is with us." No wonder they swept everything before them. A winning cry that, every time. Those who believe God to be with them are likely to win, even though their faith be a mistaken one. And this triumphant battle-cry may be yours, my young friends, in the battle of life; and yours, too, beyond a question, may be, and, assuming the conditions to be met, shall be, at once the fact which that cry expresses, and the glorious results which always follow that fact; for, in that case, God shall be with you, and through him shall you, without a doubt, trample down all your enemies.

A Winning Battle-cry.

Here, then, is our chief ally. Have God with you, and the victory is a foregone conclusion. The question arises, therefore, How shall his presence be secured?

To have him with us at all, we must have him within us; and in order to this, there

What is Necessary to put God on our Side. must be a voluntary and complete submission of our will to his will. If he is not our all, he will be nothing to us. We can not serve God and mammon. To all appeals for compromise the answer comes back, that memorable answer which Grant gave in the late war: "I will accept no terms but unconditional surrender."

OLIVER CROMWELL.

In this battle of life the first object of our great Captain is to garrison that weakest, most exposed, and most important of all positions, the human heart. That secured, there is a chance for us; that neglected, there is no chance. Hence

The Great Strategic Point in Life's Battle. it is at this point that true religion always begins. We do not put it on, we get it in. It is not a profession, it is a possession. And the terms upon which this possession comes to us are those of unconditional surrender.

When a choice has been made, and we have put ourselves, by repentance and faith, squarely on the side of God, he immediately arrays himself on our side, and the first thing he does is to regenerate our natures and to lift up within us the standard of his spiritual presence. Then the enemy, when he comes, finds the citadel in which he had hoped to establish his own camp, already occupied.

It is just as it was in the war Elisha had helped the King of Israel to carry on so successfully against the Assyrians. No sooner had the enemy purposed to ambush at a certain point, than the prophet, who divined their purpose, forestalled them by sending Israel's army to take possession in advance. So in the battle of life. The powers of darkness would fain establish their ambush in the citadel of your hearts. They know well the advantage of so doing. But God, who is aware of their purposes, and knows, too, how best to frustrate these hellish designs, would fain pre-empt their intended camping-ground for himself; and with this object in view, has sent out ambassadors to announce to all young people

A Memorable Campaign — What it Teaches.

that his very first, his most urgent, and most imperative command is, My son, give me thy heart.

But our hearts garrisoned, will the enemy then leave us? Ah! did Syria's hosts abandon the struggle against Israel when their chosen camping-grounds were pre-empted? What meaneth, then, that scene at Dothan, when, by the dawn's early light, the young servant of Elisha discovered that a mighty army was investing that city? So, rest assured, will it be in your case. To be truly converted is half of the battle, but it is not the whole of it. Such an experience gives you an unspeakable advantage, and it is indispensably necessary. This, however, though it makes peace within, is far from making peace without. It puts God on your side, but it does not cause either the devil or the world to look favorably upon you. Your conversion, in fact, will provoke these adversaries to sharper hostility. This for the reason that it will show them, beyond the possibility of mistake, that you are now squarely upon the side of right, and are defying them to do their worst.

After Conversion — What?

In this new aspect of life's battle, while still feeling that the best of all is, God is with you, prudence will require that you look carefully

GENERAL GRANT.

about to see if there are not some earthly alliances which offer help. Doing this, you will find other forts flying the standard of the Lord of hosts besides

Human Alliances which offer Help.

that within your own hearts, and other soldiers than yourself who are fighting the Lord's battles. Every true Church is such a fort, and in one of these you will be wise to seek refuge.

But can not we be Christians, you will ask, without being Church members? To which we answer, Why should you wish to be, when the Church is intended to help you, and has been placed in the world expressly that it might serve as one of your most potent allies? Why should any soldier expose himself, when it is possible for him to fight from behind fortifications? Or why should he rush upon the foe single-handed when there are comrades anxious to join him in the assault?

<small>Why we Need the Church.</small>

Besides, it is inconceivable that one who is truly converted, would want to hold aloof from the Church; for is it not a law of nature that like should be attracted to like; and do we not see in all the affairs of the world that men who have common interests, and are enlisted in the same cause, bivouac about the same camp-fires, and seek to cheer and strengthen one another by companionship and by a union of their forces?

So, my young friends, do n't think of trying to get along without the Church. Why should you, when the Church is such a powerful ally? How can you, and <small>Sterling Advice of an Old Sea-captain.</small> still have God with you, when the Church is the Church of God, and when its members are the standing army of his earthly Government? To change the figure for a moment, let me give you the advice of an old sea-captain, addressed originally to a young man who was moving from one city to another, and who fortunately had a Church letter to take with him. "As soon as you reach Philadelphia," said the captain, "present that letter to some Christian Church. I 'm an old sailor," he continued, "and it is my rule, as soon as I get into port, to fasten my ship fore and aft to the wharf. It costs a little wharfage," he added, "but it is a great deal better and a great deal cheaper than to leave the ship out in the stream, floating hither and thither with the tide."

Thus spoke that wise old sea-captain, and so say we. Get into the harbor, get close against the wharf. Anchor your ship fore and aft to the Church. Ally yourselves to Christian people. Throw about your lives the influences of Christian fellowship. As the best means of escaping bad company, surround yourselves with good company. That you may not float with the tide, get beyond reach of the tide. That the storms may not sweep over you, seek a refuge from the storms.

What that large stone church at Johnstown did, which was so strong that it divided the flood into two currents, that every Church does to the invading army of worldliness and wickedness. That is, it cleaves this army in twain, and thus saves those who are within it from the full shock of assaults which might otherwise sweep them to destruction. Hence the advisability and the necessity, to all who would succeed in the battle of life, of having an enrollment in the Church, of linking their destinies to the Church, and of using the Church in all possible and practical ways as one of the greatest and best of their earthly allies.

<small>Lesson from the Johnstown Flood.</small>

And now, back to the mountain-top, where Elisha and his servant stood, and where, inevitably, at this opening period of their lives, these young people are standing. **It is day-break** with our young friends. They are getting now their earliest views of what life promises to be. Of necessity the scene is a mixed one. Before them and above them are visions which inspire. Beneath are the hosts of darkness, the mighty foes which seek their ruin. Nor is this all they see. Their gaze, we trust, penetrates now into the invisible.

Another Glimpse of Life's Golden Morning.

Our effort has been to open your eyes, that you might see your defenses as well as your dangers, your allies no less clearly than your foes. Amongst the former, and very prominent amongst them, are the angels. Other helps are the good examples and the good influences that are thrown about you. Still another potential aid to a godly life is the Church, with its sweet communions, its gracious fellowship, and its union of forces. Better than all, though, is the fact which underlies, which crowns, and which effectualizes the other helpful forces, the blessed fact that God is with you. Not looking upon you from his throne in the skies, but with you. Not twenty miles away, as Sheridan was at a critical time in the late war, nor situated as Sherman was when he

Helps to Success in Life.

telegraphed to another general, "Hold the fort, I am coming;" but with you, really with you, is this God; his soul-inspiriting message being, not, "Hold the fort, for I am coming," but, "Hold the fort, for I am here;" his presence and gracious aid, moreover, making it absolutely certain that they who are with you are more than all who can be against you, and that if, in this great battle of life, you prove true to your trust, you can not fail to win a great victory.

PERFECT THROUGH SUFFERING.

V.

THE CAPTAIN WHO LEADS US.

CONTENTS.

THE DIVINE PURPOSE IN HUMAN LIFE—EARTHLY HONORS IN CONTRAST WITH HEAVENLY—THE CHIEF END OF EXISTENCE—OUR IMPERATIVE NEED OF JESUS CHRIST—PRIZES WE MAY WIN BY OUR OWN UNAIDED EFFORTS—SUCCESS WHICH MEANS ONLY FAILURE—TWO NOTABLE LIVES, AND WHAT THEY TEACH—TRUE SUCCESS ONLY BY SELF-DENIAL—WHAT IT MEANS TO ENTER THE ARMY—SHOULDERING THE MUSKET FROM PRINCIPLE—FIRST REQUIREMENT OF THE CAPTAIN WHO LEADS US—THREE INSPIRING EXAMPLES—NOBLE RESOLVE OF A BURMESE BOATMAN—WHAT OUR CAPTAIN HAS DONE FOR US—THE GREAT BLOT ON BONAPARTE'S ESCUTCHEON—HOW BATTLES WERE DIRECTED IN THE LATE WAR—PETER THE GREAT AND CHRIST THE GREATEST—ADVANTAGE OF RISING FROM THE RANKS—QUALITIES OF A PERFECT COMMANDER—ALEXANDER AND HANNIBAL—A LEADER WHO IS ALWAYS IN FRONT—"THERE'S THE DUKE, GOD BLESS HIM"—OF TWO COMMANDERS, WHICH SHALL HAVE US?—HOW AN ANCIENT CITY WAS SAVED—CONTINGENCY IN WHICH LIFE MUST BE A FAILURE.
114

V.
THE CAPTAIN WHO LEADS US.

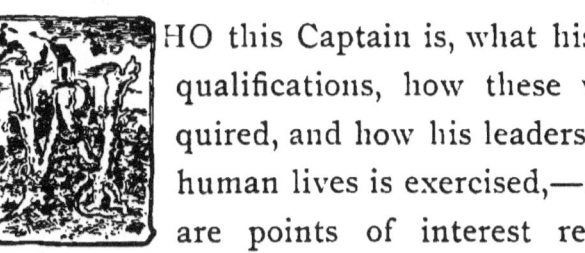HO this Captain is, what his special qualifications, how these were acquired, and how his leadership over human lives is exercised,—all these are points of interest respecting which we may fully inform ourselves from a sublime passage in that marvelous Epistle to the Hebrews, where we are told that "it became him, for whom are all things and by whom are all things, in bringing many sons unto glory, to make the Captain of their salvation perfect through suffering."

That which is here emphasized as the prime object of the Divine solicitude, and the supreme end of all God's dealings with humanity, is our salvation. *The Divine Purpose in Human Life.* Note, too, that the salvation he has in view for us is a glorious one. It is glorious because it is so complete. It meets fully all our needs, and satisfies abundantly all our noblest aspirations. Chiefly, though, is this salvation a glorious salvation, because it lands us at last in that place of glory where God himself dwells, and entitles us, as our final inheritance, to that far more exceeding and eternal weight of glory of which one of the apostles speaks.

This is what Almighty God has in view for us. His purpose is to bring many sons unto glory. This is his desire concerning every one of you, and that for which by the ministrations of his grace and through the allotments of his providence, he is constantly laboring. Of small moment is it to him whether we win or lose the baubles of honor which the world holds out to us. To us, sometimes, these minor prizes seem exceedingly desirable—so much so that the acquisition of them becomes our ruling passion and the gauge of our success in life.

Earthly Honors in Contrast with Heavenly.

So engrossed are some of us with these things, that the great prize is lost sight of altogether. As in that strikingly symbolic picture which represents a man engaged in raking stubble. Above him is an angel holding out a star-gemmed crown. The man, however, does not see this angelic visitor. So absorbed is he with the paltry occupations of this earth, that the dignities and rewards held out to him from the skies do not come within the scope of his vision. And so is it, we fear, with many in real life. What we want is success in temporal things. This battle, to most young people, means merely a struggle for wealth, for social position, for fame amongst our fellow-men, for the honors this world has to give. These acquired, we shall hold ourselves to have succeeded; these missed, we shall think we are beaten.

The apostle, however, undertakes to give us God's view of the battle of life, which, as we might naturally have expected, re- *The Chief End* verses altogether the ordinary view, *of Existence.* holding out to us, as the chief end of existence, neither worldly riches nor worldly fame nor wordly success of any description, but holding before us as the great, all-important, all-embracing prize, to acquire which all hands should be reached out and every nerve strained, the combination of blessedness which is expressed in this word salvation, a word which means, as we have already said, not only our deliverance from

sin in the present world, but our final home bringing into his own presence and glory in the world to come.

That is what God says we are to fight for; and we are further informed that to make possible the winning of that prize, Jesus Christ has been appointed our Captain in life's battle.

Our Imperative Need of Jesus Christ.

Really, this word Captain might as well have been rendered Author, and the whole trend of the passage is to show that Christ is the Author of salvation, and that this great blessing would be impossible to us without him. There is much we can do for ourselves in life, as there is also very much that can be done for us by kind friends and by adventitious circumstances. But one thing we can not do for ourselves, one thing our friends can not do for us, and that is the all-important thing; for there is no power under heaven by which any of us can be saved, excepting the power which comes from heaven.

Some prizes you may win by your own unaided efforts. We do not undervalue human capability, nor would we have our young friends underestimate it. *Prizes we may win by our own Unaided Efforts.* In worldly matters you may possibly win without Christ. Not so surely without him as with him; but you may win without him in the secular realm. Men have done this. They have scaled the dizziest heights of human achievement; they have won names for themselves which have echoed through the ages; they have attained to vast empire, and have exercised sway over millions of their fellow-creatures. Others have done this without Christ; you, possibly, may do it.

Not so well without him as with him, assuming your ambitions to be legitimate; nor, in this day when Christian principle is valued so highly, can you expect to win so easily without him as with him. But exceptional instances of such success—success achieved without the help of God through Christ—do occur even in this age; and hence we can not affirm that such a thing may not be possible in your case.

Suppose, though, you won these prizes, what would it profit you to gain the whole world if you lost your soul? What if your name be lauded on earth, if it be written not in heaven? What though you do acquire sway over others, if you bring not your own spirit into subjection? What though you should ascend the very loftiest pinnacle of earthly fame, providing you stood there at last, in hopeless solitude and in shivering apprehension, with no chariot of mercy to transport you from these earthly altitudes to the loftier pinnacles of immortal glory?

<small>Success which Means only Failure.</small>

Ah! be warned, my young friends. Have you heard of that tomb-stone over the grave of a man who died worth eight millions, the simple inscription upon which, placed there at the man's own dying request, is, "Most miserable?" Have you forgotten the death-scene of the venerable Cornelius Vander- *Two Notable Lives, and what they Teach.* bilt, whose final solace, notwithstanding all his wealth and fame, was found in those simple lines,

> In my hands no price I bring;
> Simply to thy cross I cling?

Be warned, then, by these examples. Learn from them, first, that a man may make a magnificent success of his life in a worldly sense, and at the same time, in the better and higher sense, may achieve only a miserable failure; and, secondly, learn this, that the great prize, lacking which all other prizes will be only as the trappings which decorate a funeral, but having which the soul will be rich and glorious though it have not a dollar to its earthly credit, is this grand prize of salvation through the merits of the Lord Jesus Christ.

Another suggestion of this passage which presents Christ as the Captain of our salvation, is that the path to victory in life's battle will lead, of necessity, through hardships and self-denial. Is it not *True Success only by Self-denial.*

inevitable that if the Captain could triumph only through suffering, the soldiers following him will have to carve out their triumph in the same way? This fact, however, the generality of young people ignore. They are hoping to have an easy time in life. They are flattering themselves that life's arena will be what some emigrants foolishly suppose this new land of the West will prove to them,—a place where prizes may be obtained by merely stooping to pick them up.

They have the same idea some had when they entered the army in the late war. Most of the volunteers understood what it meant; but some went out under the impression that army service would be a sort of picnic, with plenty of fun and not much to do. But O, what an awakening these had after a few days of marching in the rain, and a few nights of camping in the mud, and a few meals on hard-tack, and a few experiences of what it is to breathe the hot breath of battle! So is there, we fear, a dreadful awakening in store for some of these young people in this battle of life. They are hoping for an easy time

What it Means to Enter the Army.

of it; but the very fact that life is a battle, renders such an expectation absurd on the very face of things. Besides, how can we expect an easy time when our Captain, in fitting himself to lead us, had so hard a time, and was qualified for this task only through suffering? Is the servant better than his Lord, or is it not enough for him that he be as his Lord, and march to victory by the same rugged pathway?

Is this then, you ask—is this all you can offer us in asking us to become Christians? Have you nothing to say of the rewards of this service? But let me tell you, my young friends, that in obtruding such a view as this you reduce the Christian life to a plane where it does not belong, and give prominence to motives which should be kept in the background. Should the President of this Republic call to-morrow for volunteers for our National army, the question of true patriots would be, not, Will army service pay? but, Is the cause a just one? Poor soldiers would they make who should fight only with their monthly allowance in view. All history attests that, excepting in the rarest instances, mercenary troops can not

Shouldering the Musket from Principle.

be relied upon. Those only are worthy soldiers, and, as a rule, those only are valiant, who shoulder the musket from principle, and whose feet, as they advance to battle, keep time to the sacred music of patriotism.

So in this battle of life. Not for the loaves and fishes does God expect you to serve him. *First Requirement of the Captain who Leads us.* With no eye to either the bounty or the pension should you enlist. God's first appeal to you has reference solely to the righteousness of his cause. He wants you to serve him, not for pay, but from principle. Preliminary to all else, he asks for your affection. That yielded, the service of the life follows as a natural consequence.

The true spirit of those who would follow the banners of God is the spirit shown by that *Three Inspiring Examples.* seeker of religion who, when he was asked, had he counted the cost, replied, No, for he was determined to have it, let it cost what it might; the spirit shown by William Taylor, in his labors for the redemption of Africa, who exclaims, "O that I could multiply myself into a thousand, and give a thousand years to help Jesus!" the spirit of

Livingstone, who said once: "People talk of the sacrifices I have made. But can you call that a sacrifice which is only a small payment on a great debt? Say, rather, it is a privilege. I never made a sacrifice."

This is the proper spirit for God's soldiers, and this is the spirit which should impel these young people into his service,—the spirit of that Burmese convert *Noble Resolve of a Burmese Boatman.* who was asked if he would not devote himself to the preaching of the gospel to his countrymen. He was a boatman, earning thirty shillings a month, and the missionary frankly told him that in his new vocation he would get but eight shillings a month. "Can you go," he said, "for eight shillings?" The man sat for a time rapt in thought; it seemed hard for him to decide. But he did decide, and his decision was a sublime one, for at last he looked up and said: "No, I can not go for eight shillings, but I can go for Christ's sake."

And so is it, for Christ's sake, and not for the profit there is in it, that we would have all these young people fighting righteously and valiantly in this battle of life. There is profit in it; we do not ignore this fact; we thank God for it. There are hardships to be braved, and so also

DAVID LIVINGSTONE.

are there rewards to be won. We do not lose sight of this fact, and, on proper occasions, we do not hesitate to give emphasis to it. But what we say now is, Do this for Christ's sake; give your hearts to God, consecrate your lives to the service of God, fight manfully and perseveringly under the banners of God, for Christ's sake.

With the object of stimulating you to such a course, let us remind you who Christ is. He is the Author of your salvation. Lost by nature, by him you have been redeemed. *What our Captain has done for us.* Far away from God, his blood has brought you nigh. Children of wrath, through him you are made heirs of divine mercy. In slavery to the devil, he makes it possible for you to become children of God. Destitute of strength with which to meet your mighty foes, he gives you all the strength you need for this purpose. With nothing in prospect for the future, he opens the doors of Paradise to your vision and offers you an entrance therein.

And not only does he make salvation possible, but it is through him, and through him alone, that it becomes actual. Besides being the Author of your salvation, he is the Captain of it, the one who leads you, who cares for you, who directs your movements, who watches your foes, and works constantly to frustrate their hellish designs.

This Captain of ours does not marshal his forces for the assault, and then forsake them. He does not present victory to us as a possibility, and then leave us to carve it out for ourselves as best we can. The great blot on the military escutcheon of Bonaparte was his heartless abandonment of his brave soldiers in that memorable retreat from Moscow. But who ever heard of Christ forsaking his soldiers in the time of peril?

<small>The Great Blot on Bonaparte's Escutcheon.</small>

It was all right, no doubt, for our generals, during the late war, to watch the battles, as they did often, from a distant eminence. This was strategy; it was the best they could do. In a newspaper article we read, not long ago, of the first battle of Fredericksburg, and how Burnside, from a hill on the opposite side of the Rappahannock, with his orderlies and a telegraphic battery near him, watched and directed that battle. This, no doubt, was a wise proceeding on Burnside's part. But this Captain of ours pursues a different course altogether. His policy is to come near to us.

<small>How Battles were Directed in the Late War.</small>

Omnipresent as he is, he can be with us, and is with us—with every one of us—right where the fighting is being done. Show us where the

AT THE FRONT.

battle is the fiercest, said an ancient people, and there, surely, shall we find our prince. So, show us that spot on the great battle-field of life where Christian soldiers are most sorely pressed, and that heart of man or woman which is most fiercely besieged by the tempter, and there always shall you find our Prince and the Captain of our salvation.

Let us emphasize again the fact that this Captain of ours won his peerless distinction by suffering. He made himself competent to lead us through a world of sorrow by first passing through it himself. That he might fail in no instance to secure victory for his soldiers, he won at the outset a great personal victory. That by observation and experience he might qualify himself to be a successful commander, he first became an ordinary recruit.

For an illustration of the course pursued in this respect by the Lord Jesus Christ, we point you to Peter the Great entering the ranks of his own army, and then rising, by his own merits, to the place of supreme command; and afterwards, that he might teach the art of ship-building to his people, learning it himself by working as a common laborer in the dock-yards at Amsterdam. In that course on the part of the great Peter—a

Peter the Great and Christ the Greatest.

course of conduct at which the world has wondered ever since—behold an illustration, though a very feeble one, of what Christ did when, by his matchless stoop from heaven to earth, and by the life of conflict and hardship which followed, he made himself perfect as the Captain of our salvation "through suffering."

What soldier would not prefer as his commander, other things being equal, one who had risen from the ranks? Such a man, he would say, will necessarily have the feelings of a brother toward me. And is not that precisely how our Commander feels; for does not the same apostle who holds him up as the Captain of our salvation tell us in the same connection that he is not ashamed to call us brethren?

Advantage of Rising from the Ranks.

The captain who is made perfect through suffering will know how to sympathize with other sufferers; and not only how to sympathize, but how to succor and relieve. And is not this another characteristic of our Captain; for are we not assured that, in that he himself hath suffered, being tempted, he is able to succor his tempted followers?

And so we might go on. Portray before us, one after another, all the various qualities necessary or desirable in a perfect captain, and in this Captain not only will we match them, but we will undertake to eclipse them.

A perfect commander must have large knowledge. He must know the strength, and must be familiar with the tactics of the enemy. He should know, also, the territory on which the decisive battles are likely to be fought. He should be well acquainted, moreover, with the strength and *personnel* of his own forces. And will any one question the possession of these qualities by our Commander?

<small>Qualities of a Perfect Commander.</small>

Then, you talk of sympathy. One great commander has immortalized himself by the fact that at the close of a fierce battle, when one of his aids, by a great effort, procured him a draught of water, he waved it from him and ordered that it be given to a wounded private near by. A noble act, in very truth; and yet, compared to the sympathy and love displayed for man by this Captain of ours, not worthy to be mentioned. Had that commander, in a moment of supreme peril, bared his own breast to receive the saber-thrust intended to take the life of one of his soldiers, there would have been some ground for a comparison in the two cases; for precisely that has our Commander done, and a thousand times more.

Then, you talk of heroism—of commanders who have shared the drudgery of the soldier's toil, and have gone before him in difficult and hazardous campaigns. *Alexander and Hannibal.* You tell us of Hannibal, who led his men in carving a pathway through the mighty Alps, and of Alexander, who wielded a pick for the inspiration of his disheartened troops, as they cut their way through ice and snow into Persia. And where is there a youth whose blood did not quicken and whose heart did not throb with admiration when he first read of these instances of condescension and heroism?

Let me tell you, then, my young friends, that such a Commander is the one we follow. Ours, in fact, is a far better and nobler Commander; for occurrences like *A Leader who is Always in Front.* those just cited were exceptional with Alexander and Hannibal, whereas our Captain is always in the lead. He always goes before us. The harder the rock, the more surely will his pick be the first to smite it. The rougher the path, the more certain that his steps will be the first to tread it; for he never says, "Go into battle;" it is always with him, "Come into battle." And what that ancient king of Hungary did in one instance, when, to keep his soldiers from lying down in the snow, to sleep what must surely have been the sleep of death, he commanded them to follow him in single file, stepping in the tracks made by his own feet, and to continue their forward march only so long as he should thus make a way for them—that our Commander does all the time; for he never requires us to go where he does not himself lead the way, and asks us to pursue no path which he does not first hallow with his own steps, and light up with the cheer of his own blessed presence.

And so we might still go on enumerating the perfections of this Captain of our salvation. Think, for instance, what his power must be, in view of the fact that he received his commission from the Being for whom are all things and by whom are all things, and when he himself declares: "All power is given unto me in heaven and in earth."

Think, too, of the victories he has won. In one of Wellington's battles the lines wavered, we are told, because the commander could not be seen. Presently, however, he appeared, when one of his soldiers cried out: "There's the duke, God bless him; I'd rather see him than a brigade." And no wonder, says the one telling the story, for in him he saw a captain who had never lost a battle, and whose single presence was equal to five thousand men. And will some one tell us when our Captain ever lost a battle? We have seen pictures of Wellington in uniform, and have stood amazed at the stars and medals glittering upon his breast. But let me tell you, my young friends, that you could not adequately decorate this Captain of ours, though all the stars in the gem-spangled firmament should flash from his uniform, nor make medals enough to celebrate the victories he has won, though the gold of all the continents were melted for this purpose.

Such, briefly and imperfectly sketched, is the Captain—the skillful, powerful, courageous, sympathetic, and victorious Captain—under whose triumphant leadership we would have these young people advance to the battle of life. Take your choice, my young friends. Two commanders are bidding

Of Two Commanders, which Shall have us?

THE DUKE OF WELLINGTON.

for your allegiance,—the Savior who has redeemed you, and the Evil One, who wishes to destroy you. Take your choice; remembering this, however, that if you do not choose Christ's service, you fall into Satan's ranks as a natural consequence of your indecision. You do not need to choose his service. To be led captive by the devil, all you need do is simply to refuse the overtures of this Captain of your salvation.

Remember, too, that nothing will suffice to put you on God's side save the complete surrender to him of your hearts and lives. History relates that when the city of Capua was threatened by the Samnites, an appeal was made to Rome, and the answer being that Rome could not interfere, the citizens sent this response: "If," said they, "you will not defend us, you will, at least, defend yourselves, and from this moment we give our city to the Romans, and become their subjects;" the result being, as a matter of course, that Rome then interposed and saved them. And here, let me assure you, is the only way in which the gracious help of Christ can be secured in this battle of life which you are entering. It will not suffice merely to pray for his interposition. You must deserve it, you must entitle yourselves to it, by the complete surrender of your lives to his service.

How an Ancient City was Saved.

Remember finally, my young friends, that this Captain is a necessity to you; so much so that without him life's battle, taken as a whole, is sure to be a failure. Some battles you may win without Christ. You might possibly gain wealth without him. It is also possible for you to win a species of

Contingency in which Life must be a Failure.

worldly honor without Christ. But we are appealing to you as beings who are immortal; as those who have souls to save; as those who must stand at the judgment bar of God; as those who need pardon for sin, and the purifying influences of atoning blood to wash away the defilement of sin; as those to whose vision a door opens into the world beyond, revealing a destiny of happiness or woe which will never end. This is the stand-point from which we make our appeal to you; and keeping these facts in mind, we assure you again, with all the solemnity we can command, that without Christ you can win no success in life that will be at all worthy of either your capabilities or your opportunities, and at the same time that you can gain nothing in this world, can hope for nothing in the next.

THE BATTLE OF HASTINGS.

VI.
The Weapons of our Warfare.

CONTENTS.

Necessity of a Good Equipment—Dreadful Foes whom we can not see—A Call to Manfulness—That Noble Drummer-boy—Life's Emergencies, how to meet them—Decisive Moments in Great Battles—Why Some Days are Evil Days—How Evil Days may be made Good—Snatching Honor from the Jaws of Danger—Putting on the Armor—What our Helmet signifies—Valor in Battle, how to secure it—Stirring Address of a Wise General to his Troops—A Sure Antidote to Discouragement—Evil Thoughts; Two Methods of treating them—The Breastplate of Righteousness—Guarding the Steps, Why and How?—The Uses of Gospel Foot-gear—An Interesting Paradox—Moral Security, how obtained—The Shield we are to carry—How to resist Temptation—The Best Weapon in the Universe—Significant Conduct of Two English Rulers—Necessity of Watchfulness and Prayer—How a Memorable Battle was won—What it means to be fully equipped for Life's Warfare.

VI.
THE WEAPONS OF OUR WARFARE.

HE great difference between ancient and modern methods of warfare, and that which, more clearly than any thing else, makes the latter superior to the former, is to be found in the superior equipment which is now afforded. Men were as brave and as strong in the early days as in these, and there was as much strategy then as now. But the Greeks and Romans, accoutered as they used to be, would fall before the battalions of to-day like grain before one of our modern mowing-machines. The weapons would do it.

And if superior weapons are so essential and make so vast a difference in secular warfare, so are they equally necessary and equally potential in this higher conflict which we call the battle of life. If existence were only a dress-parade affair, the quality of our equipment would be of little importance. Life, however, is a serious business; it is a mighty struggle with foes who are so numerous their name is legion, and so powerful that their strength can scarcely be measured. This fact Paul emphasizes. We wrestle, he says, not against flesh and blood, but against the principalities, the powers, the rulers of the darkness of this world, and against wicked spirits in high places.

Necessity of a Good Equipment.

The allusion is, doubtless, to those fallen angels, with Satan at their head, of whom Charles Wesley says that

> They throng the air and darken heaven,
> And rule this lower world.

Not alone in the passage quoted, but in many other places in the Scriptures are these alluded to, and in every case the impression sought to be conveyed is that these spiritual foes are the most powerful and dangerous of any that engage us. They are more to be feared than others, because they are invisible. The advantages afforded when we

Dreadful Foes whom we can not see.

can see those who are combating us, are too obvious to need comment. But these wicked spirits in high places, led by the prince of the power of the air, we can not see. They are foes, too, of superior intelligence and of vast resources. They are not equal to God in these respects, but they are far above humanity; as much so as the angels are, for they are angels, we must remember, though they are fallen ones.

Having shown us, from the gravity of the situation, how indispensable it is that we advance to life's responsibilities with the utmost thoughtfulness and in the best possible state of preparation, the apostle we have quoted then tells us in what our preparation should consist. "Wherefore," he says—seeing you have such enemies to meet and such a battle to fight— "take unto you the whole armor of God, that ye may be able to withstand in the evil day, and having done all, to stand."

Note, as an introductory thought, that God expects you to make a bold stand in life's battle. We are to choose our ground, and then maintain it. We are to

<small>A Call to Manfulness.</small>

walk, not according to the elastic suggestions of self-interest, but by the strict rule of principle. We are to be men, not cowards. We are not to be sometimes up and sometimes down; but we are to be always up and at it. When, at Waterloo, the remnant of Bonaparte's favorite troops were asked to yield themselves prisoners, the answer came back, we are told, from those heroes of fifty battles: "The Old Guard dies, it never surrenders." And clearly is it the design of Almighty God that we shall never surrender.

That drummer-boy, captured by the enemy, and in the tent of the opposing general, com-*That Noble Drummer-boy.* manded to play for the entertainment of the officers gathered around,—let all these young people take their cue in life's battle from him. All sorts of martial music he rolled off, save one sort. That he could not render, and would not attempt. "Play a retreat," said the general; but the lad replied: "Excuse me, sir, I never learned to play a retreat."

So would the God of battles have it in our case. We are to stand, not to fall; to maintain our ground, not to run away. A retreat should we never play; but, instead of that, on every

occasion when the battle of life seems to be going against us, we must meet the crisis by sounding an advance and by rallying our forces for a fresh attack. How it impresses others we do not know, but to us the suggestion of an inspired apostle, that God's soldiers are always to stand their ground, and that, having done all, they are still to stand, has a tone of unmistakable triumph in it; for the inference we draw is, that what God intends us to do he will enable us to do, if we allow him, and that the soldier who is found always standing, and who still stands when the bugle of release has sounded and the smoke of the final engagement has blown away, can not be other than a conqueror.

<small>Life's Emergencies—How to Meet them.</small>

Another thought suggested is, that life's battle will bring to us times of special emergency. Such occasions arise in every battle. Hostilities may be in progress for days, but the crisis lasts, it may be, only an hour; in some cases only a few minutes. The successful storming of some strong position; the hazardous crossing of a stream; the dauntless stand made by a few brave men against some grand rush upon which the enemy has staked all,—these are the things, generally,

<small>Decisive Moments in Great Battles.</small>

THE WEAPONS OF OUR WARFARE. 147

which turn the tide and settle the final issue when warrior meets warrior on the field of blood. And so in the battle of life. The struggle is a never-ceasing one; hostilities will continue to the end; and yet, in nearly all cases, the fight is won or lost by the decision shown and the valor displayed in some great emergency.

These times of crisis the apostle calls "evil days;" and so they undoubtedly are in one sense. Evil days are these, because they environ us with all the powers of evil; evil, because the Evil One is so near to us; evil, because they contain within them such enormous possibilities of evil for our future life and for the welfare of our souls; evil days, because they may possibly prove to be days of disaster, days of weak yielding, days when a crown and a palm and a kingdom may be bartered in woeful exchange for a mess of worldly pottage or a moment of sensual pleasure. Evil enough are such days in this sense.

Why Some Days are Evil Days.

There is a sense, though, thanks be to God, in which these evil days may be transformed into good days; everything, as to this, depending upon our conduct in the crisis. Think of Joseph in Egypt. What an evil day was it for him when he was tempted by Potiphar's wife! All

How Evil Days may be Made Good.

the opportunities were favorable for a great transgression. But who would think of pitying Joseph when the one chance of resistance that day presented, heroically improved as it was, made him one of the grandest characters in history, and exalted him at last to leadership in a great kingdom? And those Hebrew youths in Babylon, what an evil day it was for them when the great Nebuchadnezzar held out to them the fearful alternative of bowing down to idols or being cast into the fiery furnace! Evil, because idol worship was so popular, and promised to be so profitable, and gave them the assurance of present ease and fame, while the death by fire must have seemed, in contrast, so unspeakably horri-

THE TRIAL.

ble and undesirable. But O, that evil day, what a good day they made it, when, reckless of the consequences, and caring only to do right, they threw back into the teeth of the king the heroic reply: "We will not serve thy gods, nor worship the golden image which thou hast set up!"

So, my young friends, may it be in your cases. The evil days will come, the tempter will assail, the world will ply you with its allurements, and your own hearts even, being naturally corrupt, may stand ready to betray you.

THE TRIUMPH.

Nevertheless, to you, certainly as to those who have gone before you, may every evil day be transformed into a good day—a day of holy decision, a day of triumph and of glory, and a day, perchance, which may mean for you an eternal triumph; for while every defeat weakens us, every victory, thanks

Snatching Honor from the Jaws of Danger.

be to God, makes us the stronger; while a victory under great difficulties, and with great odds against us, may possibly become, as scores of illustrious instances have attested, the deciding victory of a life-time.

Thus we are to stand in life's conflict—to stand on all the days, and to withstand in the evil days. And the apostle tells us in the same connection how this may be done. To win in this great battle of life, we must put on, he says, the whole armor of God. And now, with his words to guide us, let us examine this equipment. Let us take it up piece by piece, and see of what its various parts consist, and what are the special uses and excellences of each.

Putting on the Armor.

We begin with the head-piece; and appropriately so, for the head is the seat of consciousness. It is here that thought holds its empire. It is through the head that the senses operate and impressions are formed. A man's head is his judgment throne. There reason holds her mighty court, and there, in every normal mind, waiting the mandates of judgment and reason, sits that mightiest of earthly forces, the human will. We begin with the head. You are going into battle; the head must be protected; we put a helmet upon it; and let Paul tell us what kind of a helmet.

Take the helmet of salvation, he says; and in another place he counsels us to take for a helmet the hope of salvation. What does he mean? Why, he means that we must advance to life's conflicts having our minds thoroughly imbued with the fact that we are saved; that God has forgiven our sins, that he has put us into friendly relations with himself; that he has made us his children and the heirs of his glorious estate. That is the first conviction we are to take with us into life's battle,—that we are saved and know it; that we know we have passed from death unto life; that we know we are his; that we know we have a building of God reserved for us in heaven. Lacking such

What our Helmet Signifies.

a conviction as this, we shall advance to life's conflicts uncertain as to the side we are on, and with no distinct apprehension of the source from which help may be obtained; and how poorly any soldier would fight under such circumstances as those, it is not necessary for me to remind you.

To do his best on the battle-field, a man should know that he has a good cause. He *Valor in Battle— How to Secure it.* should see clearly the object to be gained. You must assure him, also, if you would have him do his very best, that he fights under the leadership of one who is personally interested in him. And of all these things must these young people be assured as they advance to the battle of life. Hence the necessity for this helmet of salvation, which means really the distinct consciousness of salvation.

Then, the Grecian helmet usually had a device upon its crest, something which stood for a cherished principle; and upon our helmet God has put a device representing the precious and invincible principle of hope. For a helmet, says the apostle, take, not only the consciousness of present salvation, but the certain hope of future salvation.

Ah! the Christian soldier has something to look forward to, as every soldier must have who is expected to display valor and endure hardships.

It is evening on the tented field, and the general in charge, as many a commander has done under such circumstances, musters his troops for a brief address. *Stirring Address of a Wise General to his Troops.* "To-morrow at daybreak," he says, "we shall attack the enemy." Is that all? No, he speaks again: "Let every soldier do his duty." Is that all? No, he still speaks: "Every valiant soldier shall have a reward." Nor is that all, for he speaks once more: "Let every man do his best, and we shall have the victory." Now listen to the deafening cheers and the wild hurrahs that are raised. What do these mean, does some one ask? Why, they mean that those hopeful words from the lips of a trusted commander have inspired the men with new strength and with a large increase of courage.

Now change the scene. It is not evening, but morning, on the battle-field of life. Drawn up in hostile array are a great host of young people. Their commander speaks to them. As in the other case, he first urges us to do our duty; then he reminds us of the recompense of duty done; and finally he speaks of the victory that awaits us. Notice, too, how emphatic is his language. "He that endureth *shall* be saved." He is saved and he shall be saved, day by day and hour by hour, until he is finally and eternally saved. That, in substance, is the language in which our Commander speaks, and we know that what he promises he will perform; and this hope, this assurance of final triumph, is what we are counseled to put on as a helmet.

It is by this that the mind is to be preserved from discouragement. It is this which is to make us strong when we are weak, confident when we meet with reverses, and rich when, in a worldly sense, we are miserably poor. And let me assure you, my young friends, that the man who puts on this helmet which Paul offers will indeed be rich, though he have nothing; for he will feel in the direst extremities as did that Christian woman, who, though reduced to her last crust, declared

A Sure Antidote to Discouragement.

that even that, with Christ and the hope of heaven thrown in, was too much.

Prior to his campaigns in Persia, Alexander the Great, it is said, distributed the whole of his possessions amongst his friends, and when some one asked him what he had reserved for himself, he replied that he had kept for himself the very best of all the things he ever had, which were his hopes. So with those who put on this helmet of salvation. Everything else may go, but the best will remain, for they will still have the assurance of their sonship with God, and may still exult in their hope of heaven.

Now let us look to the heart. This is the seat of life. Out of the heart are the issues of life. For our thoughts we are not always responsible. They come unbidden in many cases, and sometimes bad thoughts come to the very best of us. These, however, are sinful only when they are cherished. Afforded no encouragement, these bad thoughts will leave you as quickly and mysteriously as they came. To take a shot-gun to birds which stray upon your premises, and to build nests for these feathered intruders, are

<small>Evil Thoughts—
Two Methods of Treating them.</small>

two different courses of procedure altogether, and inevitably there will be a vast difference in the results in the two cases. Under the shotgun policy the birds are sure to take a speedy departure, while under the other form of treatment you may naturally expect them to favor you with their presence to the end of the season. And O, the many who build nests in their hearts for the nursing and nourishing of evil thoughts! Let it be remembered, however, that in all such cases we become accessory to such thoughts, and that, according to the teaching of Christ, we are as really guilty in God's sight when the wicked purpose has been formed, as when the wicked act has been done. Out of the heart are the issues of life; not out of the mind, nor out of the lip, nor out of the conduct, but out of the heart.

Inevitably, therefore, is the heart the chief point of Satanic assault. It is the key to the whole situation; hence the urgent and paramount necessity of protecting it. And so let us put a breastplate upon you, something which will render this center of spiritual life invulnerable. The apostle tells us that this breastplate must be a breastplate of

The Breastplate of Righteousness.

righteousness, and what he means is that, as the best and only protection against that which is evil, your hearts must be filled, possessed, and absorbed by that which is good. Three things are involved in the righteousness of the heart. First, our justification—that act of God's free grace by which, for the sake of Christ, he freely forgives all our sins and accepts us as righteous in his sight; secondly, a fervent, whole-souled, and unswerving attachment to righteous principles; and thirdly, such sturdy heart-righteousness as shall not fail to make the life righteous, right principles so working within us as to indicate clearly on the outside, as the face of a clock does, what time of day it is; that, too, not according to the railroad standard of convenience, but what time of day it is according to the unerring movements of the Sun of righteousness.

This is what the apostle means by putting on righteousness as a breastplate; and let me tell you, my young friends, that one thus fortified shall be more secure than even the world-famed fortress of Gibraltar is reputed to be, and as absolutely invincible to all assaults from without as was ancient Troy,—falling at last, as that city did, if fall he shall, only because in some evil moment one of the gates shall be opened, one of his good principles relaxed, and some enemy be thus admitted who shall compass his destruction from within. So that, aspiring to be perfectly secure in life's battle, your constant supplication should be, "Create in me a clean heart, O God, and renew a right spirit within me."

GREEK WARRIOR.

Head and heart protected, what now? Why, now pull on the greaves, the brazen boots; or, as the apostle says, Get your feet shod with the preparation of the gospel of peace. In ancient warfare these brazen boots were exceedingly important.

Guarding the Steps—Why and How? They were indispensable. The roads were bad in those days, dreadfully bad. Often, too, the soldier had to tramp out his own path as he advanced, the foot of mortal never having trodden the particular stretch of territory over which his march lay until that time. Occasionally, moroever, traps were set for him, as men now set traps for wild beasts, and only for the protection afforded by these brazen boots, he would have been defeated often ere the real battle had commenced.

And is it not precisely the same in the march upon which these young people have entered? Is not the road of life a hard road to travel? Are there not many rocks and thorns in it? Is it not also, in a very important sense, a new road? Millions have traversed it before us; yet, practically, every man who marches through life has to carve out his own course, and if special care be not taken, each succeeding traveler will tread upon the same pitfalls, and bruise his feet against the identical rocks that have obstructed the progress of pilgrim warriors since the world began. Hence the necessity of being shod in the particular manner suggested by the apostle, namely, with the preparation of the gospel of peace.

Notice now the uses of this moral foot-gear. The gospel affords light, and the man whose feet are shod with the gospel has light precisely where he most needs

<small>The Uses of Gospel Foot-gear.</small>

it, upon the path in which he is walking; clear light, which must of necessity make his path plain—a blazing luminary, which, like the headlight of the locomotive, shows him distinctly what obstacles are in his way, and shows him these so far ahead as to enable him to meet them without danger.

Another happy fact about the gospel is that it prepares us for life's emergencies. Those evil days of which we have spoken—they are sure to come, and if we are not ready for them, are certain to prove days of disaster to us. When, however, our feet shall have been shod with the preparation of the gospel, which means a present salvation and an ever-present Christ, we shall be ready for these evil days, and hence we shall be safe, every evil day being surely transformed into a good day.

This gospel, moreover, is declared by the apostle to be the gospel of peace; and that means that if we are shod with the gospel we shall be men of peace, notwithstanding that, in one sense, we are men of war; for in that case we shall be fighting for peace, fighting to introduce and maintain peace,

An Interesting Paradox.

fighting under the banner of the Prince of Peace, and fighting, too, in such a way that even in the thickest of the conflict we shall have the experience of peace—sweet, unbroken, and heavenly peace—in our own hearts. All this when our feet have been shod with the preparation of the gospel of peace; or, in other words—for this is exactly what is meant—when we have obeyed the gospel, and are living in the daily enjoyment of the grace it affords.

The next thing necessary is to brace the different parts of your armor together. For this purpose a girdle is offered to us. Every soldier in Paul's day wore a girdle, and it is the apostle's evident conviction that every soldier in the battle of life should wear one. He tells us, too, of what this girdle should consist. "Having your loins girt about with truth."

What is truth, you ask? What is truth? was the question originally asked by Pilate. What is truth? a minister once asked, and then, taking from his pocket a copy of the New Testament, and holding it up, he said: "My friends, this is Truth."

But Paul's idea in advising us to have our

loins girt with truth, was that we should not merely hold to the truth as it is revealed in the Book of Truth, but that we should make our lives an embodiment of truth, and that, thus, that to which we hold should hold us, by keeping our defenses perfect and by making our hearts strong. Anything false about us means just that much of weakness. We can be fully secure only when we are entirely sincere. God help us to remember this!

<small>*Moral Security— How Obtained.*</small>

It is said that upon entering the home of Tennyson you see the motto, inlaid into the pavement of the reception hall, "Truth against the world;" a sentiment which ought by right to be the watchword of every poet, of every Christian, of every man and woman, and one which we especially urge as a worthy life-motto for all these young people.

And now, with helmet, breastplate, greaves, and girdle on, what next?

Now we offer you a shield. To the Greek his shield was everything. By the skillful use of this weapon of defense, one could hold his own at close quarters against a score. It was usually oblong in shape, and so large, as a general thing, that when the soldier stooped to a kneeling posture it covered his entire body. History attests that Greek shields have turned the tide of many a battle, while there have also been instances in which, when used as a float, they have saved their valiant possessors from drowning.

This is what the Greek shield meant to those carrying it. How important is the shield which we are to bear, we may readily infer from the simple declaration, made by an inspired apostle, that it will "quench all the fiery darts of the wicked." *The Shield we are to Carry.*

Fiery darts—to what does the apostle refer in this expression? Possibly to those darts which were tipped with combustibles, and which were especially to be dreaded because, as they passed through the air, this combustible tip ignited. Or, possibly, he had reference to arrows which were dipped in poison, and which were appropriately designated by the term fiery, because when they struck the flesh, they inflamed it and produced a burning sensation, as certain serpents were called fiery serpents, because their bite produced these effects.

It is immaterial, however, from what source

this figure was drawn: that which concerns these young people is the striking appositeness of the allusion; for who does not know from experience that Satan's darts are fiery? Ah! his arrows do indeed burn us. They inflame our passions in some cases, until, as James says, they almost produce the very burning of perdition within us. These darts, however, we may escape; we may turn back to their diabolic source every one of them, passing through a perfect hail of poisoned arrows without a scratch or a taint.

How shall we do it, do you ask? Why, by stooping to our knees and by covering ourselves completely with this omnipotent shield, the shield of faith.

Yes, this is the victory that overcometh, even our faith; for when faith is in perfect exercise, when we really believe that we are the children of God, and have God for our helper and the fullness of his glory for our eternal recompense, who of us would be so foolish as to yield to temptation? In that case Satan, when he comes, finds us perfectly protected. Our shield is up, presenting a front

How to Resist Temptation.

broader and stronger than even the mighty five-plated shield of Achilles; whereas, when faith is weak and the verities of the world to come are but indistinctly apprehended, our shield is down, or, if it be not down, is defective and comparatively useless. Hence the striking pertinency of Christ's words to Peter—words which he might utter, too, with equal truth concerning every one of these young people: "Satan hath desired to have thee, that he might sift thee as wheat; but I have prayed for thee, that thy faith fail not."

Equipped thus with weapons of defense, take now the weapons of assault which are offered. They are few, but mightily effective. Here is a sword provided. It is trusty and strong; it has won more battles than all the other weapons in the universe. Different this from the swords with which, on one occasion, the English went out to do battle against the French, when, at the first blow every sword bent double because the metal was defective,—different from these swords is that we offer to you. Damascus blade was never better tempered. It flashes like the lightning, and cuts so finely that it lays open the thoughts and intents of the heart. A mighty sword it is; and yet a child could wield it against a giant, and with it one could chase a thousand, and two put ten thousand to flight.

It was this weapon for which, it is said, the child king of England, Edward VI, called, at his coronation, when he said: "Bring me another sword." They had brought him three already, as was their custom; but these did not suffice. "Bring me another," he said, "the sword of the Spirit, which is the Word of God;" and this was done, the Word of God having had a part in the coronation ceremonies of Great Britain ever since. This, too, was what Britain's present ruler held out, when asked by that African prince for the secret of England's greatness. No sword of Wellington or Nelson did she hold forth; but in her queenly hand she took this sword and said: "This is the secret of England's greatness, and this is England's glory."

Significant Conduct of Two English Rulers.

This same sword, my young friends, does the apostle hold out to those who would win greatness and glory in the battle of life. And for beating back the blandishments of the world, for bringing the flesh into subjection, and for putting the arch-fiend of the pit to flight, where is there any weapon to match this sword? That the Bible is indeed the best weapon with which to fight the devil, is taught in the most practical manner by our Savior, for it was with this that he won his personal triumph over Satan. If, however, we would use this sword as effectually as he did, it goes without the saying that we must be familiar with it as he was, must be able to quote it, must love it, must believe it, and must rely upon it.

And now, what else? Why, then we must pray; and that our praying may be timely and effectual, we must watch. This admonition to watch and pray came originally from the lips of the God-man; and how significant that he should have uttered it during the ordeal of Gethsemane, when his concern for humanity was so intense that his sweat became as great drops of blood. Notice,

Necessity of Watchfulness and Prayer.

too, how expressive is Paul's language. "Praying always," he says, "with all prayer and supplication, and watching thereunto with all perseverance."

Of the Christian warrior, furnished with every other requisite, but lacking that which is now urged, James Montgomery says:

> Undaunted to the field he goes;
> But vain were skill and valor there,
> Unless, to foil his legion foes,
> He takes this trustiest weapon, prayer.

How a Memorable Battle was Won. What school-boy has not read of the battle of Hastings, that desperate struggle in which William the Conqueror wrested the scepter of England from the hand of King Harold? And how was this battle won? By fighting, you say. Yes, and by prayer, many others affirm; for while the Saxons, who were worsted, spent the previous night in drunken orgies, the Normans, who were victorious, as all historians tell us, occupied the time in confession of their sins, and in supplicating the favor of God.

How much prayer had to do with the result in that case, we can not tell; but that it is necessary to victory in this battle of life, is beyond question. And the apostle tells us that if we would be absolutely sure of winning a great victory, we must pray always with all prayer, with all supplication, with all watchfulness, and with all perseverance.

Here, then, my young friends, are the weapons of your warfare. God help you to seize and use them!

And so, fully equipped, we send you forth. On your head is the helmet of salvation—in your head the consciousness of salvation. Over your heart is the breastplate of righteousness—in your heart the experience of righteousness. On your feet the sandals of gospel peace—in your feet the principle of gospel obedience. About your loins the girdle of truth—in your soul a supreme love for truth. One hand grasps the shield of faith; the other wields the sword of the Spirit, which is the Word of God. Your eyes are illumined with the fires of watchfulness, and out of your

What it Means to be Fully Equipped for Life's Battle.

lips proceed unceasing prayers. Thus equipped, as we pray God you all may be, we send you forth. The benediction of heaven is upon you; Christ is with you; victory is before you. And so we send you out into life's great battle, detaining you only whilst we bid you Godspeed, and whilst we remind you once more, as we did at the beginning, that it is alike your duty and your destiny to stand—to withstand in the evil day, and having done all, to stand.

A KNIGHT OF THE CROSS.

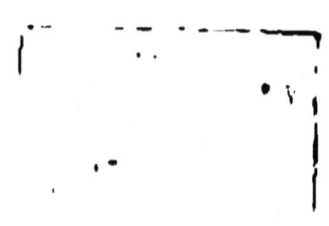

VII.
QUALITIES OF A GOOD SOLDIER.

CONTENTS.

Advice of a Veteran to Young Recruits—The Universal Desire of Young People—"Plenty of Room at the Top"—The Highest Form of Excellence—Striking Contrast between Two Kinds of Fame—Paramount Requirement of the Good Soldier—The Divine Methods of Recruiting—Hardships and Sacrifices of Army Life—Sublime Instances of Youthful Heroism—Life's Greatest Battle-field, where is it?—Appeal of Pizarro to the Castilians—Facts to be Remembered when Choice is Exercised—The Soldier's First Lesson—Consequences of Failure in Life's Battle—The Only Path leading to Happiness—Nature and Effects of True Courage—The Quality we most need—Analysis of the Courage of Luther—The Martyrs and the Great Martyr—How to fit Ourselves for Hazardous Duties—Heroism on the Field of Battle—An Old Adage improved upon—Why Some People get on in the World—The Sad Consequences of not having Grit and Grip—The Strong Pull not Enough—Characteristic Remark of Abraham Lincoln—Great Lesson taught by a Great General.

VII.
QUALITIES OF A GOOD SOLDIER.

IF one who has seen long service, and has distinguished himself on many a hard-fought field, is entitled to respectful attention when he undertakes to advise those who are just entering the ranks, then, beyond a question, is the veteran Paul entitled to the most profound respect in the counsels he offers to the youthful Timothy. Not only was it wise for Timothy to regard these counsels, but it will be equally the part of wisdom for the young people of the present day to give heed to them; for greatly as the times have changed since these words were first uttered, they have not changed to such an extent as to excuse any of us from trying to be good, nor in such a way as to exempt any who would be good from the necessity of fighting.

The special exhortation which we bring to you at this time from one so admirably qualified to give advice to those just starting in life, is that which calls upon Timothy to "endure hardness as a good soldier of Jesus Christ;" and the first thought we would urge, is that you must be soldiers of Jesus Christ. We have urged this before. There is not a chapter in this book which has not pointed to this duty; nor is there a fact in your lives which does not make this duty a necessity. You can exist without religion; but to so exist as to triumph in life, and to so triumph in life as to make death and eternity triumphant, that is utterly impossible.

Advice of a Veteran to Young Recruits.

Yet no soldier likes to be beaten. James the Second, of England, said, after a certain defeat of his forces, that he was glad it had happened, because, no doubt, it was the will of God; but we are inclined to think that James, in that instance, was something of a hypocrite. No soldier likes to be beaten. All who fight are anxious to win.

The Universal Desire of Young People.

QUALITIES OF A GOOD SOLDIER. 175

This, most assuredly, is the ambition of these young people regarding the battle of life, and it is the one thing for which you are all hoping and striving. That your hopes, however, may not prove delusive, and that your efforts may not be in vain, suffer us to remind you again that there is but one equipment which can carry you through life's conflict unscathed, and that is the armor which God supplies; but one banner that can lead you to certain victory, and that is the blood-stained banner of the cross; but one Commander who can bring you off more than conquerors, and that is Jesus. Hence the necessity of the course to which we are now urging you, and to which we have so often urged you before,—the imperative necessity of following Jesus and of enlisting in his cause without delay.

Being soldiers, then be sure that you are good soldiers. A desire to excel should characterize your efforts in every depart- *"Plenty of Room ment of life. Whatever your trade at the Top."* or profession, the principle governing you should be that what is worth doing at all is worth doing well. Is a business life your choice? Then be upright, be diligent, and plan, within honorable limits, for the largest possible success. Is the law your chosen vocation? Then go into it with the determination to adorn it, remembering Daniel Webster's saying, which is applicable at once to the legal profession and to all others, that "there 's plenty of room at the top."

Above all, though, should you strive to excel as a soldier of Jesus Christ; for the service of God is not a secondary affair; it is the chief business of your lives. Better be a good Christian, better rise in this vocation than in any other. It would pay you, indeed, and would be your duty, to seek excellence as a Christian, even though your efforts in this direction—if such a thing were conceivable—should make success in other lines an impossibility; for your qualities and attainments as a soldier of Christ are the real test-points of both character and destiny, success which does not include excellence of this description being but another word for failure, and so-called failure which does include it, one of the grandest of successes.

The Highest Form of Excellence.

Prosperity in temporal affairs is very uncertain, and at the best can be enjoyed but for a short time. You must part from it at death, if not before; and in how many instances, owing to the shifting currents and changeful tides prevailing upon life's ocean, are our temporal possessions carried away from us, leaving us dismantled and lonely and ruined, like a dismantled hulk in some great waste of waters, even while we are still living; and possibly, too, just at the time when such supports are most needed to render life endurable!

But with the good part we acquire as Christians, it is altogether different. That, we are assured, shall never be taken away from us. Other fame is but a passing show; a change of circumstances may spoil it utterly, and human caprice transform what had seemed to be a triumph into an awful mockery. But the fame acquired by the man who distinguishes himself for valiant service in the army of Christ will be as durable as the eternities, surviving alike the wreck of death and the crash of worlds; for

<small>Striking Contrast Between two Kinds of Fame.</small>

> As 'mid the ever-rolling sea,
> The eternal isles established be,
> So, through the ocean tide of years,
> The memory of the just appears.

> As in the sky the urns divine
> Of golden light forever shine,
> So, through the tempest and the gloom,
> The good man's virtues light the tomb.

If, then, it be so important that we be, not only soldiers, but good soldiers, in this army, what better can we do than offer now, for your earnest consideration, a brief summary of the qualities of such soldiers?

From the authority already cited we learn that the paramount requirement of those who *Paramount Requirement of the Good Soldier.* would be good soldiers of Jesus Christ, is that they be prepared to endure hardness. This strikes at the root of the matter. It brings us to the test immediately, just as God puts us to an immediate test when we present ourselves for enrollment as those who desire to serve him. He resorts to no deception at this crisis, nor does he indulge in any flattery. He paints no pleasing picture before us merely for the sake of getting us committed. Some governments, in recruiting men for military service, are highly culpable for the course they pursue in this respect. They set forth only the agreeable features of army life, and they grossly exaggerate even this one-sided view.

But Christ, in seeking recruits, pursues a different course altogether. The first picture he draws is a somber and rather forbidding one. Instead of empha- sizing the pleasures and rewards of his service, he thrusts upon our notice at the beginning those aspects of the Christian life which appeal to the heroic within us. His invitation is in the nature of a challenge, what he says being, "If any man will be my disciple, let him deny himself and take up his cross." *(Divine Methods of Recruiting.)*

This requirement meets us at the very threshold of his service. It follows us, too, in every succeeding step until the end is reached; for according to both our Lord's teaching and that of his apostles, the soldier of Christ must always deny himself, he must take up his cross daily, and must be prepared, as a good soldier, to endure hardness to the very end.

This is so of necessity, from the fact of his life being essentially a militant one. What else could be expected by one enlisting as a soldier? Is it not a matter of common understanding that every military recruit has many things to give up? Is he not *(Hardships and Sacrifices of Army Life.)*

compelled to forego the comforts of the home circle? Must he not bid adieu to pleasant companionships? Does he not relinquish in some cases the occupation which has brought him, perchance, a good support in life? Does he not exchange the quiet of a secure dwelling for such rest as can be snatched in tents or upon the hard ground, with only a stone for a pillow, and with no canopy above him but the overarching heavens? Must not daily intercourse with friends give place in his life to rough and deadly conflict with foes; and are not the piping times of peace, as Shakespeare says, succeeded in his experience by the stern alarms, the dreadful marches, and the wrinkled front of grim-visaged war? And if ordinary soldiering means all this, is it not inevitable that to be a soldier of Jesus Christ will entail similar hardships?

There have been instances in which young men, in order to be Christians, have been under the necessity of leaving home; and, thank God, there have been those who, when this necessity has arisen, have had the moral hardihood to meet it. The alternative being presented of giving up the

Sublime Instances of Youthful Heroism.

Church or of giving up the family hearthstone, these youthful heroes have dared, for Christ's sake, to pack up their little store of worldly goods, and go out, to take refuge, as Luther said, "under the shield of heaven," and to learn from experience, too, how grandly true it is, as David declared, that when father and mother forsake us, then the Lord will take us up.

Of course, though, such cases as these are very exceptional. But to have to break with boon companions, because their influence would be a constant temptation to us—to have to do this upon entering Christ's army—is not exceptional, but is something which is necessary in the majority of cases. Occasionally, too, men have to leave a profitable employment for the same reason. It pays well, but it is injurious to their fellow-men, or it requires them to violate some law of God, or it places them in danger from evil associations; hence it must be given up, for they are soldiers now, and, as Paul says, "No soldier entangleth himself with the affairs of this life;" and most certainly should no Christian soldier so entangle himself, if the alliance place his soul in jeopardy.

That, however, which we wish to especially emphasize, is the inward struggle of the Christian soldier, the necessity he is under of crucifying constantly the lusts of the flesh, of keeping the thoughts and desires in subjection, and of bringing his own will into harmony with the will of God. Here is the direction in which self-denial is most necessary,—here, in fact, is where it must always begin, and where, too, it must have its unremitting and triumphant continuance; for the great battle-field, after all, is in these hearts of ours, and it is there, really, that the final issue is determined. As Longfellow says,

Life's Greatest Battle-field— Where is it?

> Not in the clamor of the busy street,
> But in ourselves, is victory or defeat.

Is there then, you ask, no bright side to life's battle? Has the Christian soldier nothing that is cheering to hold in prospect? Is it, in his case, all struggle and self-denial and hardness and sacrifice? Ah! you would not ask such a question as that did you only recollect how abundantly in the promises of Christ every hardship is counterbalanced by a corresponding blessing. It is true he requires us to deny

QUALITIES OF A GOOD SOLDIER. 183

ourselves; true also that he has declared, "He that saveth his life shall lose it," and that "He who loveth father or mother more than me, is not worthy of me." But does he not also say in substance, that there is no man that hath left father or mother, or wife or children, or houses or land, for his sake and the gospel's, who shall not receive a hundred-fold in this world, and in the world to come, life everlasting?

Thus, Pizarro-like, Christ appeals to the heroic, to the love of conquest, and to the desire for glory, which is within us. Pizarro's men, we are told, had become dissatisfied. *Appeal of Pizarro to the Castilians.* He was bound for Peru; they demanded to be taken to Panama. Gathering them around him, and drawing a line in the sand with his sword, he said: "Comrades, on that side," pointing to the south, "are toil, hunger, nakedness, the drenching storm, battle, and death; on this side," pointing to the north, "are ease and safety." "But," he added, "to the south lies Peru, with its wealth; to the north Panama and its poverty. Choose now," he said, "what best becomes a brave Castilian.

For my part," he added, "I go to the South."
So, only in a far better cause, and in words
which appeal far more powerfully to that which is

PIZARRO.

noble within us, does our Leader speak. Choose
you, he says, whom ye will serve, and in what
direction your march shall lie. The world offers
you ease, attended by spiritual poverty; I offer

you hardship, which, however, shall surely lead in the end to incalculable riches. Choose, therefore, he says, which of these two courses best becomes an immortal being.

So speaks the peerless Leader who is bidding for our allegiance. Such is the alternative which, Pizarro-like, he places be- *Facts to be Re-* fore these young people, just as *membered when Choice is Exer-* they are about to take ship for the *cised.* port of their eternal destination; and we ask you, in His name—those at least who have not done so already—to form your decision here and now, and to be sure that it is a wise decision, a noble decision; remembering, as you make it, that the world, though it promises ease, does not confer it, and is not able to do so, all experience proving that a life of self-indulgence is a life of wretchedness, and that the way of the transgressor is a hard way; but that, on the other hand, the service of God, notwithstanding that it necessitates self-denial, and calls for the endurance of hardship, is still, not only a grand service, from the fact that it develops heroism and makes grand men and women of us, but is emphatically a service of freedom, a profitable service, paying well both in this life and in that which is to come—a blessed and delightful service, which exacts sacrifices only that it may confer peace, and imposes crosses, only as a preliminary to the bestowment of crowns, and requires us to walk in paths where thorns abound, only that our senses may be regaled by the beauty and fragrance of the sweet roses which also abound there, and precipitates us into trouble and conflict, only for the sake of attesting to our consciousness how very delightful it is to have the cheer and sustaining grace of an ever-present and all-sufficient Deliverer, the experience, under hardship, of every good soldier of Jesus Christ being, as one has so beautifully said:

> "It is the Lord!" Sad soul, whate'er the burden
>   That presseth sorely now,
> Whate'er the thunder-cloud which hangs its shadow
>   Athwart thy storm-clad brow,
> Fear not! No sorrow but to gladness tendeth,
>   If faith's expectant eye be upward cast;
> The darkest cloud some subtle glory lendeth,
>   And breaketh into blessing at the last.
> Soon shall thy heart in rapture be outpoured,
> And thou shalt testify, "It is the Lord."

Bearing in mind, then, that the basal quality of a good soldier is self-denial, let us now glance at some other qualities which will readily occur to us.

Every good soldier will be obedient. This is the first lesson the soldier must learn. Failing at this point, punishment will be visited upon him. Such failure, moreover, may be disastrous to others as well as to himself. It may imperil the issue of the battle; it may change the destiny of a nation. *The Soldier's First Lesson.*

Everything depends upon the soldier's obedience to orders. Occasionally, we are aware, advantages have come from disobedience; as, for instance, at the battle of Missionary Ridge. But far more frequently does disaster follow such a course. Hence the usual attitude of those in command is to condemn and punish it, even though it may be vindicated in some sense by the results. Of all soldiers must it be said, as Tennyson said of the noble six hundred:

> Theirs not to reason why,
> Theirs not to make reply,
> Theirs but to do and die.

Wellington, on one occasion, had commanded an officer to storm a certain position, and the man said it was impossible. "I asked not," said the Iron Duke, "for your opinion; I gave the orders, and expect them to be obeyed."

Not only is obedience indispensable to the well-being of the army, considered as a whole, but it is equally necessary to the comfort and welfare of the individual soldier; for it is only when such a man is obedient that he is free from reproach, free from inward condemnation and from the fear of punishment.

And if obedience be necessary in ordinary warfare, how much more so in this battle of life!

Consequences of Failure in Life's Battle. Think of the consequences of failure in life's battle. Think how much we shall lose should this battle go against us. Think, too, what losers others may become through failure on our part; for let me tell you, my young friends, that every wreck floating at random on life's ocean imperils the safety of other ships, and that every recreant soldier in life's army betrays and jeopardizes, not himself alone, but the interests of his comrades, and the holy cause for which he has sworn to fight.

In this battle, moreover, disobedience never leads to good; it is never justified by circumstances; it can never be vindicated by results. It is always evil, and it always leads to evil; for to disobey God is to forfeit the favor of God; it is to incur guilt; it is to yield to the enemy.

A WRECK.

Far from ever helping us to victory, it is in itself a defeat.

Here, too, even more certainly than in ordinary warfare, is the path of obedience the only path which can lead to happiness. A fact to be ever remembered, is *The Only Path Leading to Happiness.* that every human being is a birthright subject of the Divine Being. We can no more choose whether or not we will owe allegiance to God, than we can choose who our parents shall be, or under what flag we shall come into existence. We are all as surely and as really born under the Government of heaven, as we are born under some particular earthly Government. What is more, we must remain under this Government forever. Allegiance may be renounced in the one case; but to throw off the allegiance we owe to God is impossible; and just as no citizen of these United States can live a happy or comfortable life excepting as he shall obey the laws of his country, so is it equally futile, and even more so, for any of us to suppose that happiness can be realized, in any true and worthy sense, excepting as our conduct shall harmonize with those higher religious laws which, at the same time that they are revealed in the Bible, are enunciated with almost equal authority in the works of nature and in our own moral consciousness.

In this matter we are allowed no option by either our Creator or our own interests. If we would make life a real success we absolutely must obey the orders of our Divine Captain.

QUALITIES OF A GOOD SOLDIER. 191

In other words, we must keep the Commandments—must do the will of our Father in heaven. Otherwise we can never enter heaven, nor become the true followers of Him who came from heaven.

Another requisite is courage. Sir Horace Vere put this necessity into one sententious remark, uttered at a council of war. *Nature and Effects of True Courage.* It was during his campaign in the Palatinate. The question under discussion was whether or not an attack should be made; and some one present observing that the enemy had many pieces of ordnance planted at a certain place, and that therefore it would be dangerous to attack him, Sir Horace's reply was: "But, my lord, if you fear the mouth of a cannon, you must never come into the field."

The question arises, however, what is courage, and what are its effects? Does it follow that where courage exists all fear will depart? By no means, for the truest and greatest courage is that which takes men forward into the jaws of danger in spite of fear. "You look pale," said a man to his brother officer, as they rode together in front of a thundering battery; "you look pale; you must be frightened." "I am," was the calm and noble response, "and if you were as afraid as I am, you would turn tail." Some of the bravest soldiers who ever faced an enemy have trembled when the lines were forming, and have blanched into an ashen pallor when the first gun was fired; yet they went on and did valiantly. Braver than others are these, because, though lacking in physical courage, this deficiency is more than made up by the rich endowment they have of that higher and rarer quality, moral courage.

And let me tell you, my young friends, that such courage as this is the quality which is *The Quality we Most Need.* needed beyond all others in the battle of life. To be wholly without fear is not desirable. A species of fear is enjoined upon us in the Word of God. We are to fear Him. We are to fear the dread possibility of failure which is before us. It is with fear and trembling that our salvation is to be wrought out. We should fear ourselves, also, lest in some moment of trial our treacherous nature betray us to the enemy; and, speaking of our foes, we may well hold these in

QUALITIES OF A GOOD SOLDIER. 193

dread, considering how numerous and powerful they are. Such fear as this is becoming in us; it is wholesome; it is Scriptural; it is necessary.

Notwithstanding our timidity, however, we must still march forward, attesting our courage, as did that white-faced officer in the late war, not by the fact that it divests us of fear, but by the fact, which is far more creditable, that it nerves us to duty, and incites us to daring, and leads us to victory, in spite of fear.

What great reformer ever threw himself full tilt against the rugged front of national prejudice simply from the love of con- *Analysis of Luther's Courage.* flict, or from the delight he felt in danger? Was it so with Luther, does any one suppose? What, then, was the meaning of those struggles with himself and of those memorable conflicts with Satan, when the fiend of the pit came so near and pressed so hard as to seem really incarnate to his senses? Ah! Luther, noble soul, adopted the course he did, and pursued it in the way he did, not at all because he was without fear—for he was not—but because the sense of fear was brought into subjection to his higher sense of duty. As he himself said,

"Here I take my stand; I can do no other; God help me!" this fervent prayer for divine help constituting an expression at once of the fear he had of what might be the possible consequences of his course, and the confidence he

LUTHER AT FOURTEEN.

felt that, with God on his side, he should triumph at last, even though he might have to purchase his victory by a violent death.

And the martyrs, moreover—who supposes that they were without fear, when the wild

QUALITIES OF A GOOD SOLDIER. 195

beasts rushed upon them, or the fagots crackled at their feet? Even the courage of our Lord himself partook of this element. Even he would have excused himself at the last, but for the necessity that was laid upon him. What meant he else, when he prayed, "If it be possible, let this cup pass from me?" "Nevertheless," he added—and here is where his moral fortitude asserted itself—" nevertheless, if it may not pass from me except I drink it, thy will be done." *The Martyrs and the Great Martyr.*

O, for such courage in these young people! You will need it again and again, and again and again will you fail if you are without it. Compromises, you must remember, are not victories. You must stand up for the right at all hazards. Where Christ leads, you must follow; where duty calls, you must always dare to go. How shall we be fitted to do this, does some one ask? Why, by having the courage of the ancient reformers, the courage of that noble army of martyrs,—such courage, in fact, as that which was displayed, in every struggle against evil and at every crisis in his wonderful career, by our Divine Lord himself. *How to fit Ourselves for Hazardous Duties.*

Counterfeit courage will not do. Spasmodic courage will not answer. Mere bravado will conquer no enemies and win no respect. Self-confidence will always fail us; and as for mere brute courage—that may answer for a beast, and may serve the turn of a prize-fighter, who is little better than a beast; but in this fight for moral principles, in this battle which has been brought on by the desire of Almighty God to establish righteousness in the earth, nothing will answer save the highest form of moral courage, which we may define to be that instinct of the renewed soul which discerns the path of duty, and then, with a full appreciation of all the difficulties and dangers, and in spite of these, steadily pursues that path; never boasting, and yet never retreating; always trembling, it may be, and yet never turning aside.

Such courage had that dying soldier whose only wish at the last moment was that he might be so turned around as to make it possible for him to die as he had fought, facing the enemy. Such courage, also, had that other soldier of whom we have read.

Heroism on the Field of Battle.

He had been wounded in the late war, and his father reached the hospital just as the surgeons were taking the ball from the back of his shoulder. "I am very sorry," said the old man, "but that's a bad place to be hit." "Yes it is," said the boy, as he rolled over in a spasm of virtuous indignation; "but, father," he said, pointing to the front of his arm-pit, "the ball went in here."

Such courage as this let these young people show in the battle of life—always presenting to the enemy a full breast and a clean breast, as, assuredly, if we do so, we shall always present one which will be rendered impervious to all assaults by the breastplate of righteousness; the result being that our Father, our Heavenly Father, whenever he shall come to us, shall find us neither in the hospital, wounded and defeated, nor hidden away in any ditch of cowardice, but still on the field, still at the front, and crowned with the laurels of past victories, still carving our triumphant way in his strength to the grander victories of the future.

This naturally suggests another indispensable quality of the good soldier—perseverance. The old saying is, that all things come to those who wait. Change this so as to make it declare that nearly all the good things of both worlds are possible to those who will persevere long enough in seeking them, and you have an important statement which does not at all exceed the limits of truth. If, too, you should turn it around, the converse of it would be equally true; for without perseverance we need have no expectation of either acquiring much or being of much service to our fellow-creatures.

An Old Adage Improved Upon.

The youth who gets a good education is the youth who does not tire of studying. The girl who accomplishes herself in music, or in any other of the fine arts, is the girl who wearies not under the drudgery which long practice imposes. The great painter, who finally bequeaths to the world an immortal master-piece, is he who, perchance, toiled for years without recompense, and whose success was due far less to his genius than to the tireless industry he displayed.

Why Some People get on in the World.

And the annals of trade tell the same story, and teach the same useful lesson. To be shiftless

QUALITIES OF A GOOD SOLDIER. 199

and spasmodic is to invite failure; and almost always, when thus invited, does failure wait upon us; while, as every one must admit, there is nothing which makes success quite so sure as to choose intelligently some congenial line of work, and then persevere in the patient doing of it.

These observations apply, also, and with equal force, to moral and spiritual things. It is he only that endureth who shall be saved. To obtain the crown, we must be faithful unto death. To sit at last upon the promised throne of sovereignty and eternal dominion, we must overcome. If, however, we may trust the evidence of our senses, how many do not endure, how many are not faithful, how very many, instead of conquering the enemy, are themselves conquered!

Such as these you see one day with their armor all in place, their shield of faith lifted, and their sword glistening in the sunlight—beautiful, brave, formidable, and invincible they appear to be; and the next day armor and weapons have all gone, and the devil is leading them captive at his will. They make a brief stand, and then ensues an

The Sad Consequences of not Having Grit and Grip.

awful fall. They fight a few battles, and then, the enemy still pressing, they become discouraged, and yield to him. A transitory courage they display, such as serves for a few dashes and spurts; but they lack the grit and grip which holds on and keeps at it; and so, although they began a good work, they did not finish it.

As others have met this fate, so may you meet it; and hence our final admonition to you is to persevere. Remember, my young friends, that in life's tug, as elsewhere, it is not only the strong pull, but the long pull, that carries you through. We are to withstand in the evil day, and then we are still to stand, and having done all, we are to stand. That which makes the Germans so superior in battle to the French, is that they know how to hold on so much better.

The Strong Pull not Enough.

It was this faculty of holding on which made Grant victorious. It was this same determination to never tire until triumphant which sustained the Government at Washington in the dark days of the Civil War. Mr. Lincoln was asked if he thought the conflict would be finished during his administration.

Characteristic Remark of Abraham Lincoln.

QUALITIES OF A GOOD SOLDIER. 201

"I do n't know, sir," was his reply, "I do n't know." "What, then, is it your purpose to do?" the gentleman asked; to which Lincoln made the characteristic and significant reply, " Peg away, sir, peg away;" a course, my young friends, which, as surely as it led to victory in that conflict, will lead you to victory, if you but pursue it, in this battle of life.

Yes, here is your hope, and your only hope on the human side; and here only is your salvation, both for this world and for that which is to come; namely, in persever-

LINCOLN.

ance. One battle won, or even many battles— think not that then you have earned the right to rest, or conquered the privilege of security; for the moment you relax in zeal, or cease to pray, or call in the scouts of vigilance, that moment your situation becomes perilous, for just then the enemy is certain to appear. Always, in this battle of life, is there more to follow—more of blessing if you seek it; more of fighting whether you seek it or not.

It is related of Sir Charles Napier, that in the course of a great battle an officer came to report that he had taken one of the enemy's standards. Napier made no response. He was in conversation with another officer at the time. Thinking he had not been heard distinctly, the man repeated the intelligence. "We have taken one of the enemy's standards," he said; at which, it is said, Sir Charles turned toward him, to simply observe, "Then take another."

<small>Great Lesson Taught by a Great General.</small>

Has it been the good fortune of any of these young people to take one of the enemy's standards? If so, do not trouble to report it; in any case, do not boast of it; but take another, then another, and keep on in this pathway of conquest until the enemy's last standard shall have fallen before you, which can only be, let us admonish you, when the crisis of death has been safely passed, and when, as the result, the standard you yourself are carrying, from having flapped its triumphant folds over the last hill-top of earthly resistance, shall have been transplanted by divine hands to wave in unending triumph, as the ensign of your final and eternal

salvation, over the hill-tops of immortal glory.
And so,

> Strive, endeavor; it profits more
> To fight and fail, than on Time's dull shore
>   To sit an idler ever;
> For to him who bares his arm to the strife,
> Firm at his post in the battle of life,
>   The victory faileth never.
> "Therefore in faith abide!"
> The earnest voice still cried;
>   "Abide thou, and endeavor."

THE VISION OF CONSTANTINE.

VIII.

THE VICTORY.

CONTENTS.

AFTER-THOUGHTS OF THE GLORIFIED CHRIST—SMALL THINGS COMPARED TO GREATER—LOOKING BACKWARD—A GOLDEN THREAD OF ENCOURAGEMENT—DUTY AND DESTINY LINKING HANDS—A MECHANICAL CERTAINTY, AND WHAT IT SUGGESTS—THE TRICK OF AN ANCIENT GENERAL—AN AUGUR WE CAN TRUST—BATTLEFIELDS THAT ARE SACRED—THE GREATEST CONFLICTS OF HISTORY—CHRIST'S TRIUMPH THE PLEDGE AND MODEL OF OURS—THE "BIG I" AND "LITTLE YOU" PEOPLE—WHEN THE "BIG I" IS PROPER—DISCRIMINATING TESTIMONY OF A DYING MINISTER—THE SCENE WHEN THE KING COMES IN—LOOKING FORWARD—PICTURES OF HEAVEN BY AN EYE-WITNESS—SIGNIFICANCE OF SOME STRIKING METAPHORS—THE GLORY WHICH EXCELLETH—THOUGHTS WHICH SHOULD THRILL US—AFTER CROSSES, THE CROWN—THINGS WORTH REMEMBERING—AT LIFE'S THRESHOLD AGAIN—THE DIVINE VISITOR; HOW TO TREAT HIM—LAST WORDS.
206

VIII.
THE VICTORY.

JUST as, when a letter has been finished, we sometimes add a postscript to it, or as occasionally, in leaving home, a man will turn back to give to those in charge some final instructions, so our Divine Lord, after he had left the earth, added a postscript to what the four evangelists had written, and stooped down from his throne in glory to address a few words of final instruction to those into whose hands the interests of his cause had been committed.

Since the enactments of Calvary about ninety years had elapsed. All the apostles, with a single exception, had departed long before this to their rest in the skies. The sole survivor of that immortal band was the beloved John. To him, while undergoing banishment in the isle of Patmos, came a vision of the Glorified Christ, of which a record is afforded in the book of Revelation. It had occurred to the Savior that his Church needed some additional words both of admonition and encouragement. From his seat of supreme observation in the heavens he had discerned in his Church a tendency toward error, and the danger even of final apostasy; and the time having come to call attention to these things, and to seek to incite his followers to unswerving perseverance, he appropriately chooses as the medium of this communication that disciple whom he so fondly loved, whose genius had been kindled, and whose lips had been moved to eloquence under a divine inspiration on so many former occasions, and who, it would seem, had been kept on earth long after the allotted period expressly for this purpose.

margin: After-thoughts of the Glorified Christ.

From these last words of Christ is our last message to these young people selected. Our purpose is to sound in your ears a note of victory; and this, obviously, was the chief purpose of the Master in the vision with which John was favored. In the first three chapters messages are addressed to the seven Churches of Asia. Seven messages there are—all different in most respects, and yet, in one particular, all practically alike; for each sets forth the possibility of final triumph, and each concludes with a stirring exhortation to those addressed to see to it that that which is thus held to be possible shall become in their experience a certain and glorious reality.

If, too, we might be allowed for a moment to compare small things with those infinitely greater, it might not be inappropriate to remind you that the same peculiarity has marked the seven messages incorporated thus far into this book. *Small Things Compared to Greater.* They have differed from one another in most regards; they have been classed under different topics, and have emphasized different phases of life's warfare; and yet, in one particular, they have been precisely alike—that, too, being the same particular in which these messages to the Churches of Asia bore so striking a resemblance to one another; for we have failed in no message to hold out before you the prospect of final triumph, and have concluded no message without exhorting you, in the strongest language we could command, to the only course—that of fidelity to God—which could possibly lead to final triumph. That, however, which in former messages has been merely incidental, becomes now our principal and all-absorbing theme.

First, we urged you to enlist for life's battle by being converted, reminding you that unless this was done you would fight, of necessity, a losing battle in Satan's army; but that, enlisting under the Savior, and continuing to serve him, you could not fail to fight a winning battle. Then we spoke of the flag you ought to follow—a flag lifted up in the name of God; a flag, indeed, which God himself lifted up, centuries ago, among the hills of Judea—the blood-stained banner of the cross; an ensign, we assured you, which had been an unfailing guaranty of triumph to faithful ones since first its crimson folds opened to the sunshine and flapped defiance to the winds of opposition.

Then we admonished you of the foes you have to fight. Numerous, crafty, powerful, dia-

Looking Backward.

bolic, ever-present, and ever-pressing, we described these to be, as they unquestionably are; yet, far from leaving you in despair before these foes, we did our best to leave you with the feeling that sharp conflict conduced to heroism and nobility of character—that such a situation is precisely what is best for us, and that the harder the battle, the greater would be the recompense and glory of those who are so fortunate as to win it. Then we reminded you of the allies who are pledged to your help—the angels, the Church, the good people about you, and, better than all, God over you and Christ within you; the conclusion we reached being that they who are with you are many more and much greater than those who are against you, and that therefore, if you were only faithful, you could not fail to be successful.

Then we presented Christ as your Captain—another topic which enabled us to affirm the certainty of your final triumph. Then we described the weapons of your warfare, which, though not carnal, are mighty, through God, to the pulling down of strongholds, and which, properly used, would

A Golden Thread of Encouragement.

enable you, as we emphatically showed, to quench all the fiery darts of the wicked. Then, in the chapter immediately preceding the present one, we sketched for you a picture of the qualities of a good soldier, declaring these to consist mainly in moral hardihood, obedience, courage, and perseverance—qualities which we then declared, and do now again declare, seldom fail to insure success in even the temporalities of life, and never fail to make us successful in the moral and spiritual phases of life's battle.

Thus the pleasing idea of final victory has been under treatment in one way or another constantly. Every topic has had in it a note of victory, and every appeal has been really a presage of victory. Now, however, that you may be divested entirely of fear, and may advance to life's battle with a confidence that shall have no doubt whatever in it, we bring you in this last message a distinct promise of victory, and what is more, a glowing picture of the glory which will follow victory, this promise emanating from the lips, and this picture being drawn by the hand of our Divine Lord himself, whose soul-inspiring words are, "To him that overcometh

THE VICTORY. 213

will I grant to sit with me in my throne, even as I also overcame, and am set down with my Father in his throne."

Do not forget, my young friends, that in this battle your duty and your destiny alike are to overcome. It is no experiment you are trying. Upon the divine side of our lives there is no uncertainty, not the shadow of a doubt, as to the final result. The dubious clouds which presage failure come into view only when we look at the human side. No man was ever lost because God could not save him; no man was ever defeated by Satan through either a defect in his armor, or a failure of any of his weapons, or a scarcity of heavenly supplies; but every man who is defeated in this strife falls a victim to his own perversity; and every one who is lost meets this awful fate for the simple reason that he would not come to Christ for life in the first instance, or else did not come to him afterwards for the grace needed in the evil days of temptation. *Duty and Destiny Linking Hands.*

We are placed in this world expressly that we may overcome it. It is God's purpose that we shall overcome it, and all his illimitable resources are pledged to our help for this end. It is a familiar saying that everything in the heavens is for the sole benefit of the earth. Probably this is not true in its fullest sense. The planets which give us light, and whose powers of attraction keep our earth moving within its orbit, give light, we may well suppose, to the inhabitants of other worlds. Be this as it may, however, that everything in God is for the benefit of the earth, and that all the resources of infinite grace laid up in the heaven of heavens, are at the command of the inhabitants of the earth for their personal salvation—of this no believer in the Bible can have the slightest doubt; and this fact is what we have in mind in affirming so positively that it is possible for us to be victors in the battle of life, and that our duty and our destiny alike are to overcome.

These young people all know what a suction-pump is. When this device first came into use, *A Mechanical Certainty, and what it Suggests.* a mechanical expert, who had great faith in it, was questioned about it by the owner of a boat, who doubted its efficacy. "Suppose," said this doubter, "suppose the appliances all perfect and all in place, and yet suppose the pump to not bring up water, what should you say in that case?" "I should say," said the expert, "that something was wrong with the pump." "But suppose," the man continued, "suppose nothing was wrong, and still water did not come—what should you do then?" "Why, then," said the man, with an emphasis of triumph, "I should go on deck and see if the river had not run dry." And so, in any alleged case of a faithful Christian failing in any time of need to obtain a sufficiency of divine help, should we want to know if the river of salvation had not run dry; and until you could prove to us that God had ceased to be God, or had forgotten to be good, we should be compelled to maintain that that man's defeat was attributable, not to a lack of grace, but to some defect in the appliances, to some failure on his own part to communicate properly with the inexhaustible source of grace.

And being destined to victory in advance, as we assuredly are, both by the divine nature and the divine promises, what an advantage do we possess in this fact! To men fighting an ordinary battle such an assurance would count so favorably as to be almost sufficient in itself to win the battle.

Better this, in ordinary warfare, than either good weapons or impregnable armor; better than overwhelming numbers. How very desirable this is, we may learn from that ancient general, who, in consulting an augury, practiced a trick upon his soldiers. Upon his own hand he wrote the word victory; then, snatching from the priest the liver of the bird he had dissected, and pressing it upon his palm to receive the imprint he had prepared, he held it up before his men, to whom the word victory meant, of course, that the gods foretold their success in the conflict upon which they were entering, the result being that these men displayed prodigies of valor which without such a stimulus would have been impossible. Who does not recall, moreover, the vision of Constantine, that shining cross which seemed to appear in the heavens, with the motto girdling it, in letters of flame, "*In hoc signo vinces*" (by this sign conquer); and who, that remembers the incident, needs to be reminded of the mar-

The Trick of an Ancient General.

velous influence of that vision upon Constantine's army?

But think of this, my young friends. If a promise of victory based upon a trick could spur those pagan hosts to triumph, and if the vision of Constantine, *An Augur we can Trust.* which was probably, at best, only the pleasing fancy of a devout and over-excited brain, meant so much to him—if these things could produce such prodigies of valor, and could enable those believing in them to win such glorious victories, what influence for good should not these words of Christ produce? for that which these offer is no trick of either a faithless priest or a false commander; nor is it any mere sign of triumph which has come to us through a dream, or has been evolved from an excited fancy; but that which is here offered to all these young people is an assurance of triumph from the lips of God himself—an utterance, in fact, which links your triumph to that of your Savior, and makes it just as certain that you will overcome, the necessary means being used, as that he overcame.

This latter thought let us emphasize a little.

Let us take you for a moment to some of the battle-fields trodden and hallowed by the bloody *Battle-fields which are Sacred.* but victorious footsteps of the Son of God. That battle of the Wilderness let us call up, the opening battle of Christ's ministry, in which the arch enemy laid siege to his intended victim from every point of vantage, and tested his armor at every joint and crevice; with no more effect, however, than when the mad waves of old ocean dash themselves to pieces against the rock-bound coast. Think, too, how he walked through this world's corruptions, stooping to the foulest, that he might lift them up, and not disdaining to eat with sinners; yet still, according to the testimony of both friends and enemies, being without sin himself, and a total stranger to even the semblance of guile. Remember, too, his heartless treatment by those from whom he had deserved only gratitude and kindness—how he was crossed and thwarted in the good he tried to do, and cursed and reviled for the kind words he spoke, and how still, through it all, he gave blessings for curses, and continued, to the end, to overcome evil with good!

THE VICTORY. 219

Then, in the battle of the garden behold him,—weak nature shrinking from the terrible ordeal, and yet, his indomitable spirit forcing nature to do its bidding—compelling the reluctant hand to press against lips which would fain have been excused from drinking it, the bitterest cup which human wickedness or divine justice ever compounded. And then see him in the last battle, in Calvary's stupendous struggle, that awful contest from which, as though he might be fearful of the result, the sun hid his face, and in sight of which Old Nature, who ne'er had looked upon the like before, sobbed and trembled until her rocky bosom burst open in an earthquake. Behold him there, my young friends,—the flesh weaker than ever, and yet the spirit stronger than ever; in such agony that he begs for a drink to quench the burning thirst his sufferings have produced, and yet in such triumph that he invokes forgiveness in behalf of those who are slaying him; his great heart ready to break from the pressure of woe it is undergoing, and yet, the burden steadily, heroically, and triumphantly borne—the whole of it, even to the

The Greatest Conflicts of History.

last huge weight which fell upon him when his father's face was hidden—the whole of this burden steadily, heroically, unflinchingly borne, until at last he confounds the powers of hell, and thrills every angel's heart with rapture, and reassures the frightened king of day, and calms the tremors of the shaking earth, by that final exclamation of triumph, "It is finished!"

Behold your Savior, my young friends, under these circumstances, in all the full glory of a Christ's Triumph the Pledge and Model of Ours. triumph which has been the astonishment of the world ever since it was won; and then, while your hearts still throb with the ecstasy of that triumph, and the tears fall, as they surely must, in grateful recognition of the blessed fact that Christ did all this and bore all this out of sheer love for poor sinners, let us remind you of still another blessed fact, which is, that surely as he overcame, may you overcome, and that, furthermore, your triumph may be as complete, as enduring, as grand, and as glorious as was his; and we tell you this, bear in mind, upon the highest possible authority—no less than Christ's own words, and no other than his very latest words, which

THE VICTORY.

distinctly suggest, as do many other passages of Scripture, that Christ's victory is not only a sure guaranty of ours, but is also the shining pattern according to which, assuming that we are faithful, our victory is to be modeled.

It is worthy of note, too, that, according to the same passage, the battle of life is to be carried to a triumphant conclusion under Christ's personal supervision.

Considering who is speaking, how refreshing it is to find the personal pronouns scattered so profusely through this passage! For a speaker to obtrude his own personality upon an audience is, usually, quite offensive. We do not like the "big I" and "little you" people, as a general thing. When, however, it is Christ who is speaking, and when the theme upon which he expatiates is human salvation, this form of expression is just the thing; nothing else would suffice; and that which disgusts us in other cases, in this case challenges our gratitude and thrills our souls.

<small>The "Big I" and "Little You" People.</small>

That commander who ordered his men to advance, and said, as he bade them go, " Recollect that I am with you "—we are rather inclined to smile at him; though his men did not, for to have with them in the battle such a general as he was, meant a great deal to those who knew him. So, likewise, are we inclined to see only egotism in the memorable words uttered on a certain occasion by Sir Philip Sidney. He was directing a small body of men in an assault upon a much larger one. "Now," said he to his soldiers, "let every man engage one other man, and I will take care of the rest;" and, read in cold blood, the promise seems to savor of vanity. Possibly, though, it was proper enough under the circumstances which called it forth; certainly it had a good effect.

But O, think of the effect when our Commander utters such words! No smile of contempt in that case, but streaming tears of grateful adoration. No thought of egotism, but the feeling welling up within us that he who thus expresses himself has a right to speak in such language. And is it not an unquestionable fact that our Commander has thus spoken, telling us to advance to the conflict, and then immediately adding, "Lo I am with you—always with you;" thrusting

When the "Big I" is Proper.

us into fierce battle, and assuring us, as he does so, that if we but do our part, he will take care of all the rest?

Notice, too, how he emphasizes this fact in the passage we are considering. To humanity he refers but once, to himself five times. Ah! it is Christ who has this matter in hand. He it is through whom you are to overcome. He it is who shall personally attend both to your triumph, and to the bestowment of the glory which is to follow that triumph, his promise being, "To him that overcometh will I grant to sit with me in my throne, even as I also overcame, and am set down with my Father in his throne."

It is worth noting, moreover, that the final reward of the successful Christian soldier is described in this passage as a grant— Discriminating Testimony of a Dying Minister. something bestowed, not in the form of a reward, but as a free gift. And what could harmonize more perfectly with the facts? Who ever merited, or ever could merit, the unspeakable dignity of sitting down with the blessed Christ in his throne? Ah! that good man, Thomas Hooker, was right. Stretched upon his death-bed, and nearing the end of a life spent in devoted service to God and humanity, some friend visiting him remarked, in his hearing, that he was going now to receive the reward of his labors; upon which, however, the good man, it is said, roused himself to observe, as his streaming eyes turned gratefully toward heaven: "You are mistaken; I am going only to receive mercy." And he was right; for whilst it is true that we can enter heaven only when, by hard and successful fighting, we have won our entrance, we still do not by any means obtain this entrance because we have won it; we obtain it solely through the merits of Christ.

Really, we do not win heaven in any sense, but Christ wins it for us. So that, as that eloquent Scottish preacher has so forcibly said, when the King of that fairest of all lands shall stand up among the nobles of his kingdom and demand by what power they gained their possessions, the response will not be as, when one of England's kings asked this question of his nobles, and when immediately a hundred swords were unsheathed, and all present, with one voice, replied, "We won our lands by these, and by these are we

The Scene when the King Comes in.

determined to hold them;" but the response, when the question shall be asked in heaven, "Who are these, and whence came they?" will be, "These are they which came out of great tribulation, and have washed their robes in the blood of the Lamb; therefore are they before the throne." Not by the blood of battle, but by the blood of Christ; their inheritance gained not by their own swords, but by the sword of the Spirit, and their united and unceasing acclamation being, in consequence, "Not unto us, not unto us, O Lord, but unto thy name be all the glory, for thy mercy and thy truth's sake."

It is perfectly in order to speak of heaven, because the message we have brought you from the lips of Christ speaks of it. To be sure, the name of this place is not mentioned; but what else can be thought of when the promise is given by Christ that we shall sit down with him in his throne? Allow us therefore, under Christly sanction and guidance, to transport you for a time away from the smoke and sweat and blood of the stern battle-fields, where you are now contending with mighty and desperate foes, to the place

Looking Forward.

of peace, of triumph, of coronation, and of eternal glory.

Ah! how often does the soldier dream at night that he is at home! How often does the dew,

THE SOLDIER AT HOME.

falling on his upturned cheek, seem to him as the dewy kisses of that sweet wife, and the rough blanket he hugs to his shivering form like the tender embrace of those darling children! He is still upon the battle-field, really, and will waken again, erelong, to the stern realities of conflict; but in his thoughts is he sharing, for a little time, in the sweet joys of home. The cruel war is over, and he has his reward in children's kisses, in a fond wife's endearments, in the respect of neighbors, and in the gratitude of his country. Similarly would we have these young people imagine for a few moments that the warfare of life is ended, and that, amid the ecstasies of that better home in the skies, they are enjoying at last the far more exceeding and eternal reward which the King of heaven is preparing for his soldiers.

How entirely proper it is to encourage ourselves in life's battle by thinking frequently of what awaits us at the end, let Christ bear witness to us in these messages to the Churches of Asia. There are seven of these messages, and each concludes by sketching for the Christian a rough outline of what his final glory will be. Each lays upon us the obligation to overcome, and each tells us what will follow such a triumph.

In the first message Christ says, "To him that overcometh will I give to eat of the fruit of the tree of life," that which is here promised being a blissful immortality,—Paradise regained; a restoration to our souls of the innocence and happiness enjoyed by our first parents while they reposed in the shade and partook of the fruit of the life-giving trees of the first Eden. In the next message the promise is that he that overcometh shall not be hurt of the second death; another promise of everlasting and ever-blessed life; for the second death means the punishment of perdition, and, of course, those unhurt of this will escape perdition, and attain to a destiny directly opposite thereto. The promise of the next message is that he that overcometh shall eat of the hidden manna. A portion of manna was preserved in the ark, and the ark, with all its sacred contents,

Pictures of Heaven by an Eye-witness.

THE ARK.

had been lost. But the triumphant soldier of the cross is promised the felicity of recovering this inestimable treasure. That which has been hidden is to be brought out for his entertainment, the idea being that in our eternal fellowship with Christ we shall enjoy, in a spiritual sense, all that was symbolized, not only by the manna, but by the other contents of the ark, and, in fact, all that was symbolized in the entire Mosaic economy. We are also, this promise says, to receive a white stone; this in token of our acquittal at God's judgment bar, and in allusion, doubtless, to the fact that in ancient times stones were cast by judges to announce their verdict, a black one meaning guilty, and the white stone symbolizing innocence and consequent triumph.

In the next message the promise is, "He that overcometh, to him will I give power over the nations;" meaning, doubtless, that he shall share in Christ's power over the nations when all the nations shall have been brought into submission to him. "And I will give him the morning star," continues the Savior, a glory second only to his

<small>Significance of Some Striking Metaphors.</small>

own glory, as the radiance of that bright luminary which heralds the day is exceeded only by the clear light which the day itself ushers in; an idea which sustains the sublime fancy indulged, in one of his flights of eloquence, by Bishop Ames, when he pictured the conquering saint entering the gates of Paradise, and imagined that he heard God saying to the most exalted of spiritual intelligences: "Stand back, Gabriel; stand back, Michael; stand back, all ye angelic hosts, and make room for one who must be next only to myself."

The promise immediately following speaks for itself. It needs no explanation. "He that overcometh the same shall be clothed in white raiment; and I will not blot out his name out of the book of life; but I will confess his name before my father and before his angels." Then, to the Church at Philadelphia he says: "Him that overcometh will I make a pillar in the temple of my God, and he shall go no more out;" an allusion, probably, to the great pillars—one representing strength and the other beauty—which adorned the temple of King Solomon. "And I will write upon him," he continues, "the

THE VICTORY. 231

name of my God;" this to indicate his exalted rank; "and the name of the city of my God, New Jerusalem;" making his appearance so glorious that none shall fail to recognize him as a citizen of the place of glory. "And," he adds—this, no doubt, being infinitely better than anything else promised, though what it means we shall not presume to speculate upon—"and I will write upon him my new name."

Such, briefly sketched, are six of Christ's messages, six of the pictures he draws with the object of setting forth the glory which awaits the triumphant Christian soldier; *The Glory which Excelleth.* and it would almost seem as though, in the effort to do justice to this theme, language had been beggared and the choicest gems in the whole realm of metaphor pressed into service. And still, in this seventh message, does he promise us something further, and something grander as well; for if it means so much to have the tree of life, and the white stone, and the hidden manna, and the stainless garments, and the morning star, and the new name—if these things, these representations of heaven, image to us so much that is desirable and glorious, then what must it mean, or, rather, what must it not mean, of all the dignities possible or conceivable, to be permitted to sit down

LOOKING FORWARD.

with Christ in his throne, even as he is set down with his Father in his throne!

Ask us not to describe what this means, for

THE VICTORY. 233

in presence of such ineffable glories human thought is paralyzed, and human language awed into silence. If you could tell us what Christ's throne is, we could then tell you what your throne will be in the event of your being faithful to Christ. If you should picture out the strength, the majesty, the scope, the durability, the grace, and all the glory appertaining to his dominion when it shall be complete in the end of time, we could then draw a picture of the sovereignty, the dominion, and the glory to which the faithful Christian will finally be exalted; for we should borrow the outlines of the second picture from those given in the first, and should have abundant warrant in Scripture for so doing. Not that our sovereignty will be equal to that of Christ; but it will be like his; it will, in fact, according to Christ's own teaching, be a part of his.

Such is our final destiny. O, think of it; think of it till your cold hearts get warm; think of it till your failing strength shall *Thoughts which* wax into renewed vigor; think of *Should Thrill us.* it till your feeble courage shall be nerved to fresh exertion, and until all thought of hardship and all liability to discouragement shall be cast behind you forever; think of it till your eyes shall glisten with tears of gratitude, and until, as you shall seem in blissful anticipation to be taking part in those august ceremonies, your lips shall open to exclaim in astonishment and in trembling ecstasy,

> How can it be, thou Heavenly King,
> That thou should'st us to glory bring;
> Make slaves the partners of thy throne,
> Decked with a never-fading crown?
>
> Hence our hearts melt; our eyes o'erflow;
> Our words are lost; nor will we know,
> Nor will we speak of aught beside—
> My Lord, my love was crucified.

After Crosses, the Crown. As yet, however, we are not there. Not upon the throne yet, but still upon the battle-field. Ours not the palm of triumph at present, but the consecrated cross. Yes, crosses here; but shall we not cheerfully bear them in view of what is to follow? Who can help thinking of that dear little child, the daughter of a woman who was suffering imprisonment because she was a Christian, and of the happy thought which led her to cut out a lot of small paper crosses, and pin them here and there upon mamma's dress, and then make a great big crown, and put that above the crosses, on mamma's head? A happy thought it was, indeed, and a heavenly child must she have been who conceived it; for there, precisely, is the true view of life, the identical view which Christ holds out to us; our destiny here being crosses; then, however, after the crosses, above the crosses, and entirely obscuring by its surpassing glory all trace of the crosses, a great crown of sovereignty and eternal dominion.

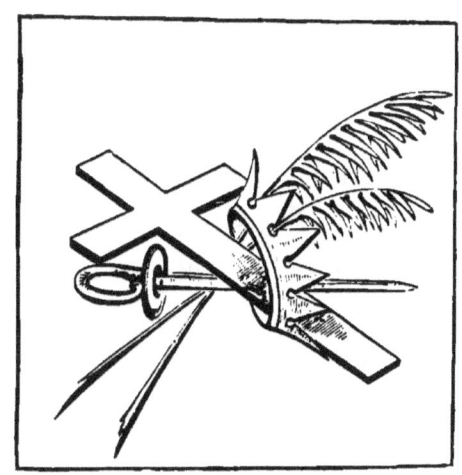

So, let us be cheered, let us be stimulated; remembering this, that our destiny is linked indissolubly to that of Christ; that as regards this world, it is not so much what we can do as what he can do; and that, as regards the next world, it is beyond a question that if we are one with him in suffering,

<small>Things Worth Remembering.</small>

and one with him in triumph, we can not fail of being one with him in glory; everything thus, as to both worlds, depending upon our getting near to him, and still, with each succeeding day, getting a little nearer; our experience in this respect patterned after that of the venerable man who said he could not tell exactly why he expected to get to heaven, only from this fact, that as he neared the end he seemed all the time to be getting a little nearer to Jesus; the result being, if this shall indeed become our experience, that when the end is reached, we are certain to be with Jesus—are certain to sit down with him in his throne; and seeing him as he is, and being so closely identified with him, are certain also to be like him; this latter constituting the one fact with reference to our destiny which shines out in the firmament of Scripture more distinctly than any other, and which is more precious than any other; for, as the beloved John says, "It doth not yet appear what we shall be; but we know that when he shall appear, we shall be like him, for we shall see him as he is."

And now, having taken you forward to the end of life's battle, we shall close by taking you backward to its momentous begin- ning. Observe, too, how closely these extreme points of existence are connected with each other. What a striking instance of this have we in that message of Christ upon which the present chapter is based; and how well does this striking fact serve our purpose in this final appeal! That which we desire you now to notice is, that in the verse immediately preceding the one in which sovereignty and dominion are promised to those who shall overcome in this battle of life, the blessed Christ, who gives us that promise, presents himself as a suppliant, begging at our hands the favor of being allowed to save us. "Behold," he says, "I stand at the door and knock." At what door? we instantly inquire. Tell us, O tell us, without delay, at what door does he knock?

<small>At Life's Threshold Again.</small>

How can any of us help asking this question, or be other than deeply anxious about the response it shall evoke?

<small>The Divine Visitor—How to Treat Him.</small>

Suppose it were announced to you that Prince Bismarck, retired from office recently amid the tears of a grateful nation, was in your city, and was knocking somewhere for admittance and recognition. Who of us, in that case, would not at once say: "Where is he? Where is this distinguished man? Let us see him, let us know him, and let us give him a welcome." Need I remind you, however, that there is really in your midst a personage of far greater distinction than the greatest statesman of Europe? O, it is the Savior, the Prince of Peace, the Lord of lords, the King of kings. He it is who has honored with a visit, not one city alone, but every city; and the door at which, in all the majesty of his Godhead and in all the tenderness of his humanity, he is knocking for admittance, is the door of every human heart.

O, wonderful condescension, and wonderful, most wonderful, the results depending upon your action in the premises! Open your door to his steps, and he will open to you the door of heaven. Admit him here, and he will admit you there. And now, with an awful sense of the stupendous issues involved, we pause to ask, Who will do this—who will let this dear Savior come in?

Heaven grant that you may all admit him; remembering, my young friends, as we have re- peatedly reminded you already, Last Words. that to end right you must begin right; that to fight under Christ's banner you must enlist in his cause; and that the only possible way to secure for yourselves a final seat upon his throne, is to give him a seat upon your throne—the throne of your pure and undivided affections—saying to him, as you still feel the pressure of his gentle hand upon your sensitive natures, and are moved and thrilled by the pleading and melting tones of that tenderest voice which ever spoke to mortals:

> God calling yet! Shall I not hear?
> Earth's pleasures shall I still hold dear?
> Shall life's swift passing years all fly,
> And still my soul in slumber lie?
>
> God calling yet! And shall he knock,
> And I my heart the closer lock?
> He still is waiting to receive,
> And shall I dare his Spirit grieve?
>
> God calling yet! I can not stay,
> My life I yield without delay;
> Vain world, farewell; from thee I part;
> **The** voice of God hath reached my heart.

www.ingramcontent.com/pod-product-compliance
Lightning Source LLC
Chambersburg PA
CBHW021350230426
43666CB00006B/468